Farewell to Christendom

FAREWELL TO CHRISTENDOM

The Future of Church and State in America

Thomas J. Curry

OXFORD

UNIVERSITY PRESS

2001

OXFORD
UNIVERSITY PRESS

Oxford   New York

Athens   Auckland   Bangkok   Bogotá   Buenos Aires   Cape Town
Dar es Salaam   Delhi   Florence   Hong Kong   Istanbul   Karachi
Kolkata   Kuala Lumpur   Madras   Madrid   Melbourne   Mexico City   Nairobi
Paris   Shanghai   Singapore   Taipei   Tokyo   Toronto   Warsaw

and associated companies in
Berlin   Ibadan

Published by Oxford University Press, Inc.
198 Madison Avenue, New York, New York 10016

Oxford is a registered trademark of Oxford University Press

Library of Congress Cataloging-in-Publication Data
Curry, Thomas J.
Farewell to Christendom : the future of church and state in America /
Thomas J. Curry.
p. cm.
Includes bibliographical references and index.
ISBN 0-19-514569-0
1. Church and state—United States. 2. Freedom of religion—United States.
3. United States. Constitution. 1st Amendment. I. Title.
BR516.C93 2001
322′.1′0973—dc21   2001016313

1 3 5 7 9 8 6 4 2

Printed in the united States of America
on acid free paper

For L. B. M.

Given the number of books about American Church-State relations, a reader might reasonably ask why another is needed. Most of the historical background surrounding the First Amendment has been known for decades, and it is unlikely that any major new historical evidence will be discovered. However, the fact that a great deal of historical evidence has been available does not mean that it has been accounted for or used well.

The following work expresses my puzzlement about how so many writers on Church and State could continue to ignore what to me is the plain consensus of the evidence of the way Americans in the 1780s understood establishment of religion. I have long been fascinated that writers who accord authority or even reverence to James Madison for his part in enacting the First Amendment also adhere to an interpretation that sees him as not quite knowing what he was doing, as needing some correction and guidance, or as silently changing his mind on a crucial Church-State issue.

Above all, I have sought to escape from the ideology that has engulfed discussion of Church and State wherein authors are as predictable as night and day, and seminars and symposia as ritualized as a minuet. I have tried to approach the subject of Church and State by way of a historical method that avoids the adversarial and advocacy approach, derived from the legal system, by which writers select evidence that bolsters their position and either ignore or discount contrary evidence. My objective is to account for the totality of the historical evidence as well as for the motivation of the historical actors.

My intellectual journey to this point has been a long one. It has taken me years to escape the conventions that dominate thinking on Church and State, and I suspect many readers will also find it difficult to abandon them. However, given the alternative of remaining mired in the present stalemate, I hope the following will enable them to escape it.

ACKNOWLEDGMENTS

In writing this book, I have incurred many debts of gratitude. To Professor Edward M. Gaffney, Jr., I extend my deepest appreciation for his excellent comments on the manuscript and for some careful legal advice. John Coleman, S.J., read an earlier version with great care and insight. Anne Dunn, I.H.M., gave me unfailing confidence, encouragement, and helpful comments. My friend Monsignor Royale Vadakin gave me the benefit of his usual shrewd and practical judgment. My sincere thanks to Bishop George H. Niederauer and Bishop Stephen E. Blaire for their friendship, as well as their continued interest and positive comments on my endeavors. I am deeply grateful to Cardinal Roger M. Mahony for his constant kindness. The ever-abiding care and welcome of Marita and Thomas Broderick, Enda and Therese Curry, and Brid and Bernard Sharkey have sustained me through the years. My thanks as well to Cynthia Read, Theo Calderara, and Robert Milks of Oxford University Press for shepherding this manuscript to publication. For her endless patience and invaluable editorial asistance, I am eternally grateful to Lois B. Marquez.

CONTENTS

Farewell to Christendom

INTRODUCTION

More than two centuries ago, by deciding against maintaining an established church, the United States embarked on a new and radical course. It not only broke with its European roots; it departed from previous human experience. Until that time, for most of humankind—with such notable American exceptions as Rhode Island and Pennsylvania—the idea that a society could be maintained without its governing authority upholding and promoting a central belief system would have been inconceivable.

This work celebrates the historic decision embodied in the First Amendment. However, it also delineates and reflects on the continual pull of the past, the persistence of the notion that in the absence of a core religious belief system sustained by the State, freedom or even society itself is in danger of destruction.

Those who would return to state-supported religion, who seek the functionality of an established church while simultaneously attempting to avoid its inherent coercive features, are easily recognizable, most clearly to their opponents. The position that government may promote religion for the purposes of strengthening public morality has a long history, and it still attracts a good deal of support in America.

Those who perceive that the First Amendment set a different direction for America also respond to the tug of history, although in a less obvious way. Although they eschew the concept of state-supported religion, they often fail to recognize that they themselves would have government impose a nonreligious ideology as a central organizing force for society. In an attempt to guard against the tyrannies of the past, they would not only have judges disallow religious legislation but would permit them to evaluate the religious consequences of secular legislation, that is, whether such laws aid or hinder religion. Instead of limiting the role of government, this approach would confer on it powers equal to those of the most authoritarian regimes of modern times by enabling judges to review virtually all legislation according to a religious criterion. Many who rightly laud the achievement of the United States in dispensing with established religion would nevertheless endow government with power to determine not just the function of the State but the proper sphere of the Church. They would not only have government define and arrange what is political but declare, as well, the boundary between the sacred and the secular.

Failure to sufficiently understand the radical break with the past represented by the First Amendment has resulted in the amendment's being viewed through an ideological mindset that it was enacted to avoid. My own experience tells me that readers will often seek first to determine whether the author of a work dealing with the amendment is "separationist" or "accommodationist" and then proceed to read the historical evidence the work discusses solely in the light of that determination.

The influence of such ideology in discussion of the First Amendment has resulted in the triumph of a literalist approach over a historical one. The fundamental tenets of both sides of the existing ideological divide can only be maintained by discounting historical evidence that does not comport with positions already established and by a fervent adherence to metaphors—such as the "wall of separation" or "the naked public square"—rather than to a more careful and practical search for definable terms.

This dominant literalism is characterized by a preponderance of assumptions that the First Amendment was enacted by a people whose ways of thinking matched those of modern Americans and who dealt with the same Church-State issues that prevail in America today. As a result, studies of the amendment often treat it as a statement intended to provide answers at the time to specific questions in a distant future rather than as a proclamation of principle by a people unable to envisage its application beyond the limits of their own experience.

This work proceeds from an understanding of the amendment as a limiting, self-denying ordinance restraining government, a mandate that the State will exercise no power in religious questions, that "Congress shall make no law" in that domain of human experience. Religious freedom proceeds from government's leaving people to decide on their own religious beliefs and practices. Some would, with the best of intentions for society, now have government return to the practice of sponsoring and promoting religious beliefs and observances. Others, equally well intentioned, would guard against the abuses of the established religions of the past by endowing government with power to corral religion, to locate the Church behind a wall or barrier of the State's making.

In reality, the First Amendment is about government's lack of power. It is no more a mandate to promote religion than it is one to create a boundary defining the sphere and activity of religion. Rather, it embodies a new way of arranging government, the full understanding of which is still emerging. The gravitational force of Christendom, built up over more than fifteen hundred years, remains strong. The silence of those empty spaces created by the disappearance of established churches can still disturb or even terrify those who are not religious. Nevertheless, the great American experiment still challenges religious believers to realize that the denial of government power over the Church resulted not from a depreciation of religious belief but from a profound appreciation that religion was too important to be left to politicians, too precious and necessary to a vibrant society to be made the tool of government manipulation. The following pages are offered as a guide to that developing understanding and to a realization that the limited, secular, non-ideological government mandated by the Constitution and the First Amendment provides the best hope for Church and State in the new millennium.

ONE

SETTING THE CONTEXT

The refusal of modern governments to uphold the teaching, customs, ethos, and practice of Christianity, either Catholic or Protestant, has resulted in the end of "Christendom." In popular commentary, this phenomenon is sometimes equated with post-Christianity. Judging whether people are now more or less Christian than previously would require a sweeping assessment of Christianity and a broad comparison of past and present. By contrast, however, the evidence for the end of Christendom, the system dating from the fourth century by which governments upheld and promoted Christianity, is readily observable.

This book revolves around two major proclamations of the end of Christendom. The first originated in the Protestant tradition and came by way of the First Amendment to the United States Constitution, enacted 1789–1791.* The second emerged from the *Declaration on Religious Freedom* proclaimed in 1965 by the Second Vatican Council of the Catholic Church.[1]

---

* The First Amendment reads: "Congress shall make no law respecting an establishment of religion, or prohibiting the free exercise thereof; or abridging the freedom of speech, or of the press; or the right of the people peaceably to assemble, and to petition the Government for a redress of grievances." For purposes of this work, the term "First Amendment" will refer only to that provision of the amendment that deals with religion.

The Present Crisis

This work proceeds from the conviction that the interpretation of the earlier of these two proclamations, the First Amendment, has reached a point of deep crisis. Historical scholarship dealing with the background and enactment of the amendment is at an impasse, and judicial interpretation of it is in a state of disarray. This crisis was precipitated in 1947, when the Supreme Court set a direction for discussion of the First Amendment founded on assumptions radically at odds with the amendment's historical origins as well as with human experience.[2] Since then, scholars and judges have followed the Court's lead and even added to its original misassumptions. As a result, each successive year has seen the discussion and debate surrounding the meaning of the First Amendment carried ever farther from its historical source and ever deeper into the thickets of confusion.[3]

Modern Church–State discussion has been based on the following misassumptions: that the free exercise of religion is the equivalent of religious toleration; that members of the First Congress disputed the definition of establishment of religion; that the Free Exercise and No Establishment provisions of the First Amendment serve differing purposes and exist in tension with each other; that the amendment deals with government aid to or hindrance of religion; and that it requires government to maintain a neutral stance between assisting or impeding religion, between religion and nonreligion, and between differing religions. These misassumptions proceed from a mindset essentially derived from Christendom. Modern attempts to build a wall, to draw a line, to define a boundary between Church and State replicate the perennial struggle of Christendom to separate the secular and the sacred into their proper spheres, even though the First Amendment was designed to end that long conflict by proclaiming an end to Christendom in America.

The second proclamation of the end of Christendom, the *Declaration on Religious Freedom,* is of much more recent origin than the First Amendment. Therefore, its implications have been much less discussed. However, just as the consequences of the amendment are still being worked out by modern American society, so, too, the changes affecting Church and State inherent in the *Declaration* are still emerging, and some of these are discussed and anticipated in the following pages.

This work provides a new paradigm for the understanding and exploration of religious liberty.[4] It argues that much of the current confusion in discussion of religious liberty can be traced to habits of mind that persist from the Christendom of the past. It explores and interprets the First Amendment as it was meant to be, a departure from the thinking that had preceded it for nearly fifteen hundred years.

Christendom: A Brief History

Christendom is usually traced back to the Roman emperor Constantine, who, in 313, legalized Christianity by the Edict of Milan and thereafter involved himself intimately in the affairs of Christianity, building churches and even convening a council to define the nature of Christian belief. By the end of the fourth century, Christianity had become the official, established religion of the Roman Empire. Subsequent governments of the Christian world would continue this tradition of promoting, cooperating with, or controlling religion.[5] With the disintegration of the Roman Empire in the fifth century, Christianity assumed an even greater importance, in that it became the principal cultural and civilizing force in the chaotic world of what had been the western part of that empire. Even as new political entities began to emerge, the predecessors of modern European nation-states, Christianity continued to provide the principal overall unifying force.

Religion played such an enormous part in the post-Roman world that Christianity, citizenship, and society became intermingled and indispensable to each other. Until the formation of some of the American colonies in the 1600s, the idea that government could exist without being grounded in Christian belief and practice was inconceivable. Therefore, full membership of society and adherence to Christianity became synonymous. To abandon Christianity or to practice a form of it not sanctioned by the civil authority put one outside the pale of society and often involved forfeiting life itself. Even after the Protestant Reformation begun by Martin Luther in 1517 precipitated a major division within Christianity, both the worlds of Catholicism and Protestantism continued the traditions of Christendom inherited from the past, although each shaped the religious foundations of society to its own theological views. Before the reign of Constantine, religion and government had been united, with the emperor as both head of state and chief priest. Edward Gibbon wrote that the "various modes of worship which prevailed in the Roman world were all considered by the people as equally true; by the philosopher as equally false; and by the magistrate as equally useful."[6] Only when Constantine legalized Christianity in 313 and the Christian Church claimed a separate sphere of influence did the problem of separating religion and government into their proper spheres arise. Although Christendom distinguished between and separated the sacred and the secular powers, it conceived of society as an organic whole and envisaged both as cooperating in a joint task, each fulfilling its proper role. Ideally, both would work together for the common good. The Church, as the spiritual authority, would anoint the ruler and bind subjects to his power by an oath of loyalty. In turn, the ruler, as the secular authority, would protect the Church, promote the true religion as defined by it, and punish dissenters. The two powers would work hand in hand to promote a culture, a legal system, and a way of life based on Christian beliefs. Such a system provided little room for dissenters, and non-Christians existed only on its fringes.

In the world of historical experience, however, separating the two powers and defining the proper limits of each proved impossible. Disputes between the two bedeviled Christendom and consumed the energies of both in endless conflicts. Sometimes these conflicts took place on a local level, between a bishop as a representative of the spiritual authority and a feudal lord or prince. Sometimes they involved much of Christendom, as when the pope and the whole Church came into conflict with a king or a combination of civil rulers. A penitent Emperor Henry IV in 1077, kneeling in the snow at Canossa before a dominant Pope Gregory VII, and the murder of Thomas Becket in Canterbury Cathedral in 1170 following his conflict with King Henry II remain as enduring images of the struggles between the two powers.[7]

Several of the American colonies broke this cycle of conflict between Church and State by refusing to establish any church or religion. In the wake of the American Revolution, the newly formed United States solved the seemingly eternal problem of determining the proper spheres of the sacred and the secular by simply opting out of the debate. The United States Constitution defined American government as secular, as having no power at all in religious matters, that is, religious belief, practice, doctrine, or devotion.[8] Henceforth, government would confine itself to its own limited and specified powers and leave religion entirely free to define itself and its activities. Government would neither exercise power over nor make decisions about religious matters, neither define religious truth nor punish religious error. Thomas Jefferson explained that the federal government was endowed with "civil powers alone" and could not prescribe "any religious exercises" or "assume authority in religious discipline."[9]

The Problem a Bill of Rights Posed

The framers of the American Constitution saw themselves as devising a government of limited and specified powers. Power over religion was not given to the government but rather reserved to the people themselves. Thus, they believed that a Bill of Rights protecting religious liberty and other fundamental rights was unnecessary: Why prohibit the exercise of powers not granted? In James Madison's estimation, the new government possessed not even the "shadow of right" to meddle in religion.[10] This American historical development is clear and largely uncontested.

People in the individual states, however, when presented with the new Constitution for ratification, were not content with an implied guarantee of fundamental freedoms; they wanted explicit protections for them, and they demanded a Bill of Rights. Alexander Hamilton, writing in the *Federalist Papers,* opposed the idea. He considered a Bill of Rights not only superfluous but downright dangerous. Its provisions would contain "various exceptions to powers not granted; and, on this very account, would afford a colorable pretext to claim more than were granted. For why declare that things shall not be done which there is not power to do?"[11] Madison, on the other hand, realized that without the guarantee of a Bill of Rights, the Constitution would never gain the votes needed for ratification. Moreover, on a personal level, he believed that unless he committed himself to such a bill, Virginia Baptists would oppose his bid for a seat in Congress.[12] Therefore, he devoted himself to the enactment of one.

Ensuing history has vindicated the wisdom of both the people's and Hamilton's positions. Given the enormous controversy over the meaning of the First Amendment's explicit prohibition of government power in religion, one has to wonder what would have been the fate of religious liberty had that prohibition remained only an implicit assumption. Nevertheless, what Hamilton predicted has also come true. The wording of the amendment designed to specifically prohibit the exercise of such power has become the source of a modern controversy about what kind of power the government is enabled to exercise over religion.[13]

Wrong Assumptions

Much of the present difficulty surrounding the meaning of the First Amendment arises from the largely unexamined assumption on the part of judges and scholars that the amendment actually created a right and that the courts are the guardians of that right. The Supreme Court has come to see the amendment as primarily intended to protect the right of individuals to the free exercise of religion rather than to limit government action. It has held in the past that freedom of religion holds a "preferred position."[14] Some justices and commentators maintain that government may promote religion, may use it, for example, as a "unifying mechanism" for society, as long as such promotion is not coercive. Others argue that government may accommodate religion by removing "a discernible burden on the free exercise of religion." Still others would envision the Court as the protector of "personal liberty," as an energetic guardian of the religious freedom of minorities.[15] Virtually all commentators would agree with Justice Antonin Scalia's assertion that "free exercise of religion means, first and foremost, the right to believe and profess whatever doctrine one desires."[16]

On the contrary, however, the First Amendment is first and foremost a limitation on government, a command that "Congress shall make no law. . . ." The amendment did not create religious liberty, and the government and the courts are not the guarantors of that liberty or of the liberty of individuals. Rather, the amendment is a guarantee that the government will not impinge on the religious liberty citizens already possess by natural right or human dignity. The proper role of judges is to ensure that government stays within the limits of its power as defined by the Constitution and does not intrude on religious liberty by attempting to make decisions about religious matters.

As Hamilton so shrewdly understood, affirming a negative is as diffi- °
cult as proving one. He foresaw the danger involved in a provision that
forbade the use of a power that did not exist:

> They might urge with a semblance of reason, that the Constitution
> ought not to be charged with the absurdity of providing against the
> abuse of an authority which was not given, and that the provision against
> restraining the liberty of the press afforded a clear implication, that a
> power to prescribe proper regulations concerning it was intended to be
> vested in the national government.[17]

Indeed, the modern debate about the historical meaning of the First
Amendment is characterized by what Hamilton anticipated. Historians
have recast the discussion that surrounded the enactment of the amendment into a struggle between those who wanted to endow the new federal government with power in religious matters and those who did
not. This recasting has resulted from projecting into the past a definition of establishment of religion based on logical analysis, instead of
empirical historical evidence. In reality, the original discussion constituted a debate over how to make explicit a guarantee on which all the
members agreed—that the federal government had no power in religious matters—rather than a dispute about the meaning of establishment of religion.[18] Moreover, much modern academic advice about the
First Amendment, as well as an important judicial approach to it—
whether a law has the primary effect of aiding or hindering religion—
would endow government authorities and judges with power to make
decisions about religious matters.[19]

Logic over History and Experience

Chapter 2 reviews the historical background of the First Amendment
and explains how the presuppositions of current Church-State scholarship have led modern discussion away from the context of that background. This historical exploration has been guided by the insight of
Oliver Wendell Holmes, Jr., who, in writing about the Common Law,
declared, "The life of the law has not been logic: it has been experience."[20] Some of the conclusions modern scholars draw about the historical meaning of the First Amendment are logical; they are plausible

and reasonable, but they are not historical. They fail to reflect how those who enacted the amendment thought. Rather, they are founded on abstract logical deductions drawn from statements made at the time and on textual analysis of wordings carried out apart from their historical context.

History provides a storehouse of evidence about the original meaning of the First Amendment. Most of the states in drawing up new constitutions addressed the issue of Church and State. Two of them in particular, Virginia and Massachusetts, settled on diametrically opposing arrangements in that regard. In reaching their respective positions, each involved its citizens in passionate, popular, and widespread debate about the relationship between government and religion. Because of that involvement, we can know as much about what ordinary Americans in those states believed about Church-State relations in 1789 as we can know about perhaps any other subject in American history prior to the advent of modern polling.[21]

In an extraordinary failure to keep in mind the historical context within which the First Amendment was enacted, scholars and judges have for more than half a century misread the debate in the First Congress about how to word a provision explicitly denying the government power in religion. In assuming how Americans of 1789 defined "free exercise of religion," they have equated that concept with religious toleration, that is, that government may not coerce citizens in their religious beliefs.[22] The development of religious liberty in America, however, emanated from the radical Reformation idea that true reform could be brought about only by grace, by the conviction of believers guided by the spirit of God. Any government interference in religious matters would inevitably manipulate and corrupt the Church. Thus, religious liberty had come to mean religion exercised voluntarily and free from government intrusion, even if it proceeded from the best of motives. By 1789, this way of thinking, together with a belief that religious freedom was a "natural right" reserved to the individual and not delegated to the state, formed the basis of American understanding of the free exercise of religion.

Because modern scholarship has missed the significance of this development of the meaning of free exercise, it has focused primarily on the topic of establishment in dealing with government sponsorship of religion. Although Americans at the time were unanimous in their understanding of "establishment of religion" as a government preference for one church, sect, or religion, modern scholars have projected into the past not only a division among them as to its meaning but also a struggle between differing parties over their supposedly respective definitions of the term. [23] They base these historical misassumptions on the fact that some senators made several attempts to word the amendment dealing with religion by using the following or a similar formula: "Congress shall make no law establishing any particular denomination of religion in preference to another."[24] From this fact, scholars have drawn two purely logical inferences. One group among them argues that the framers saw a difference between a preferential establishment of a single state church and a nonpreferential establishment of several or all churches and prohibited both. An opposing party contends that the same framers defined an establishment of religion simply as a government preference for a single church and therefore, in banning such an establishment, were not objecting to nonpreferential government assistance to many or all churches or to religion in general.[25]

This projection of the modern notion of nonpreferential government sponsorship of religion into the past has disconnected contemporary discussion of the meaning of the First Amendment from the amendment's history. The notion is a purely present-day intellectual construct, quite at odds with the reality of the time to which it refers. Not a shred of actual evidence exists to verify that when the Framers prohibited the establishment of any one religion, they implied either support for or opposition to nonpreferential government sponsorship of several religions.

Nor does the historical record provide the slightest proof that members of the House or Senate engaged in the kind of struggle latter-day writers attribute to them. Their concerns were entirely different. Some of them thought that enacting amendments wasted precious time that should have been devoted to more important items than banning the use of nonexistent powers.[26] Others possibly wanted the amendment worded to reflect the common usage of the time and to employ phrases from contemporary state constitutions.[27]

Moreover, members of the First Congress utterly lacked a motive for doing what modern scholars claim they were doing. Not only is there no evidence of anyone who wanted to give the federal government power in religious matters, one cannot even imagine who might have been motivated to do so. Federalists thought the government was fine as it was; anti-Federalists feared and loathed the new government and had no wish to confer more power upon it. All agreed that the new government was powerless in religious matters.

The modern nonpreferential inference is also at odds with religious experience and human behavior. The *Federalist Papers* saw religion as a prime source of faction and of possible oppression by majorities. The Constitution was written by men who understood that people in power tend to support their own beliefs, ways of thinking, culture, and religion at the expense of others, and that they do not tend to be so disinterested, noble, fair, or impartial as to support all religions. Religious liberty, Madison explained, would be preserved by mutually suspicious religious groups checking and balancing each other rather than by the virtuous behavior of those in government.[28] His thinking in that regard accurately reflects religious experience. By nature, religious belief is exclusive. The more devoutly people believe, the more they are convinced of the truth of their own beliefs and disinclined to approve of public support for those whose tenets they consider wrong, abhorrent, or perhaps dangerous.

Establishment of religion has always involved a government preference. That has been the human experience and probably always will be. It is certainly how Americans of 1789 understood the term. The notion of nonpreferential government authority in religion can only survive in an abstract, logical world quite cut off from the realities of human history. Nevertheless, participants in the modern Church-State debate have continued to rely on logic because for so many years it held out to proponents of competing points of view the possibility of a decisive victory. Over the decades, however, this hope has steadily receded. Time and prolonged controversy have demonstrated that only by ignoring huge amounts of countervailing historical evidence can either side maintain its respective certainties.

The constant use of history to shore up partisan positions regarding the meaning of the First Amendment has brought into question the usefulness of history at all in explaining its meaning. As often happens in protracted campaigns, one of the principal casualties in the long-drawn-out conflict is the cause for which the struggle began. Just as the Wars of Religion that tore Europe apart for more than a century following the Reformation led to disillusionment with all religious belief, so the controversy regarding the historical meaning of the First Amendment has led to an increasing suspicion that history has little power to reveal its meaning. Having posed it nonhistorical questions, proceeding from unproved hypotheses, the disputants have become disillusioned because history cannot answer them.[29]

Disparity between Principle and Practice

Chapter 3 examines the discrepancy between thought and action in American history following the enactment of the First Amendment. Although Americans, in approving the amendment, thereby proclaimed the end of Christendom, they by no means ended all the customs, assumptions, and practices associated with that system. The majority of the population at the time simply assumed government practices of a religious nature that were acceptable to them represented no more than the common coin of universal culture.

By contrast, in contemporary France, revolutionaries ended Christendom in a completely different and radical fashion. Seeing themselves as devising a blueprint for the future, they attempted to systematically dismantle every manifestation of it.[30] Americans, however, worked out their principle that government had no power in religious matters in response to experience. They had determined what religious liberty meant to them by dealing with the conflicts and problems they encountered in their various states. Having solved those difficulties and disputes, they assumed that the matter of religious liberty had been settled. Living as they did in a religiously homogeneous society, they thought of their experience of religious liberty as normative for all times and places. Thus, by the time the amendment was enacted, Americans had by and large reached the limits of their imagination as to the implications of the end of Christendom for their society. The amendment seemed to contemporaries to mark the end of a process, not the beginning of one—to represent the very capstone of freedom achieved. For the vast majority of Americans, who enjoyed an unprecedented level of religious freedom, it surely was. In a nation composed almost entirely of Protestant Christians, few could imagine that the principle of religious liberty they espoused embodied the potential to further transform society and religion as they knew them.[31] Indeed, several decades had still to pass before the advent of Catholic immigrants would force them into awareness of the full significance of the end of Christendom.

From the 1820s on, Catholics emigrated to the United States in ever growing numbers, bringing with them a culture and understanding of religion and a worldview vastly different from those they encountered on their arrival. Religious practices that to Protestant Christian America were intrinsic to civilized living seemed to Catholic Christians an imposition of sectarian belief and practice. As a result, the next 150 years witnessed a prolonged controversy about the nature of America, the role of religion in the nation, and the meaning of religious freedom. This protracted conflict would lead to the further unfolding of the religious liberty embodied in the First Amendment and would alter America forever.

The history of Catholicism in America has been written largely from an assimilationist perspective that portrays Catholics coming to a new country, experiencing great difficulty adjusting to it, being subjected to much harassment and bigotry, but gradually adapting, acclimatizing, and blending into American culture. This historical image is generally pessimistic and inclined to view Catholics negatively, as failing to adjust quickly enough to democratic ways, to make a mark on American culture commensurate with their numbers, or to form an intellectual tradition.[32] By contrast, this book advances a transformationist viewpoint. Particularly in matters of Church and State, it perceives Catholics as providing the essential counterbalance that Madison had realized would be necessary to the preservation of religious or any other freedom. Catholics challenged the blend of religious culture and political power they found in America and ultimately helped enormously to dismantle it.[33] They contributed in a major way to the fuller achievement of what the First Amendment proclaimed—the end of Christendom. Catholics not only adjusted to America; they transformed it and helped recreate it. Over time, drawing upon their experience in a new land, American Catholics were able to convey to the Catholic Church at large the meaning and the importance of religious liberty. They played a crucial part in bringing about the *Declaration on Religious Freedom,* Catholicism's proclamation of the end of Christendom, issued in 1965 by the Second Vatican Council. Like the Americans who brought about the First Amendment, however, Catholics tended to see the *Declaration on Religious Freedom* as the end, rather than the beginning, of a process. The still unfolding implications of that *Declaration* may well produce results not necessarily anticipated by those who helped bring it into being.

Court Decisions Past and Future

Chapter 4 looks at decisions of the United States Supreme Court. The purpose of this review is to test the compatibility of decisions already made with the interpretation of the First Amendment as having the unitary purpose of prohibiting government exercise of power in religion and to illustrate how the Court might address future cases. The chapter does not attempt to provide an extensive analysis of the reasoning the Court has used to justify its Church-State decisions. The argument of the book is that a lack of historical understanding has hampered the Court in its efforts to make a coherent connection between its decisions and its justification of them. This is not to argue, however, that the Court's failure to make such a connection calls for a wholesale revision of those decisions. I agree with a recent commentator's assessment that "on the whole, the Supreme Court has moved in the direction of freedom."[34]

Much of the difficulty with modern Church-State discussion arises from the persistence of habits of mind of Christendom that inevitably draw government into religious matters. Some would have government promote specific religious beliefs or practices, even over the objections of minorities, from the conviction that without such support civilized society cannot hope to survive. Others would favor a less specific public religion, a type of civic religion. All connect with the belief inherited from Christendom about the necessity of government-sponsored religion.

On the other hand, many of those who would guard against the ills of Christendom adhere to rhetoric and reasoning that is more consistent with some of the most authoritarian governments of modern times than the government envisaged by the American Constitution and the First Amendment. Instead of viewing the amendment as depriving government of power, they see it as conferring on government enormous authority to determine the sphere of religious practice and confine it behind a metaphorical *wall* of the State's making.

One of the Court's tests for legality has been whether a statute has the primary effect of aiding or impeding religion. This is an essentially religious question, and engaging in it involves the justices in a pretence that they have power and responsibility in religious questions, even though in their official capacity they are not competent to resolve them. What helps or hinders religion is a matter for religious believers to decide. Secular authorities have no power to make such judgments. Rather, what the Court must determine is whether the statute in question constitutes a valid exercise by government of its constitutionally enumerated powers.

Because the habits of mind inherited from Christendom include the notion of separating competing parties, powers, or values, modern scholarship has become preoccupied with the question of neutrality. Scholars proceed from an assumption that the government must find— and remain on—neutral ground between aiding and hindering religion, between the Christendom of eighteenth century England and New England or the anti-Christendom of the French Revolution. In demanding neutrality between aiding and inhibiting religion, many constitutional scholars invite the Supreme Court to make its home in the dangerous no-man's-land between these two.[35] The concept of neutrality is not a useful one for Church-State relations. It conjures up an image of government maintaining an impartial attitude, withholding assistance equally from all— and refraining from impeding any— of the parties to a conflict. The language of incapacity, want of mandate, or lack of competence would better describe the situation of government with regard to religion in America. The First Amendment renders government powerless, not neutral, in religious affairs. The role of the Court is to say what is secular, not what is religious; what is within the limited powers of the State, not what assists or impedes the Church. It has not been designated to solve the problem that bedeviled Christendom by settling the proper boundaries between Church and State, between the sacred and the secular.

Summary

One major source of the modern crisis in Church-State discussion is that as presently formulated, the two principal contending coalitions would each interpret the First Amendment as justifying the exercise of government power in religious matters. One side would grant government noncoercive or nonpreferential power over religion. However, the concept of nonpreferential government power over religion is a purely logical invention—supported by no historical experience—that would perpetuate Christendom. In American history, majorities have always decided that what was acceptable to them was noncoercive or nonpreferential as far as others were concerned.

Opponents of this nonpreferential position, encouraged by extravagant judicial rhetoric in the past, would have government solve the problem of Christendom by assuming the power to determine the proper roles of Church and State. They would give the government authority to build a figurative *wall of separation* between Church and State, to decide what was good or bad for religion, what aided it or hindered it. Behind that *wall,* the government would allow the free exercise of religion. This group would, as the Supreme Court has said, use the secular power to "create a complete and permanent separation of the spheres of religious activity and civil authority by comprehensively forbidding every form of public aid or support for religion."[36]

The argument of this book is that the First Amendment addresses itself solely to the power of the State. Focusing on the separation of Church and State or on exercising neutrality in religious matters only involves government in attempting to achieve what Christendom sought vainly to accomplish. Within the meaning of the First Amendment, the free exercise of religion is properly understood as religion exercised voluntarily and without any interference by government in religious issues. Free exercise of religion is an inalienable right reserved to the people—not a gift of the government, but the sovereign right to be left alone, untroubled by any incursions of the State into religious matters. That is what free exercise meant at the time the amendment was enacted. By establishment of religion, the Framers understood a government preference for one religion or church. In prohibiting an establishment, they were specifying and excluding the manner in which, from time immemorial, governments had exercised power over religion and violated its free exercise.

Because modern scholars tend to assume that the First Amendment created religious liberty and that the government is the guarantor of that right, they bring the Free Exercise and No Establishment provisions of the amendment into conflict.[37] On the one hand, they see the government as assisting individuals in the free exercise of their religion, and on the other, they see the provision against an establishment as forbidding government to assist churches and religion. However, when the amendment is viewed in its original context as a requirement that

"Congress shall make no law," that the government will exercise no power in religion, this tension is clearly resolved.

The key to finding more coherence between Church-State decisions and the historical meaning and purpose of the First Amendment lies in an understanding of the latter as a limitation on government. The amendment requires government to evaluate laws in terms of their effect on the State, not the Church. The statement that "Congress shall make no law respecting an Establishment of Religion or prohibiting the free Exercise thereof" was designed for the single and unitary purpose of expressing the government's lack of power over religion. Its intent is to confine the State to its appropriate role. Attempts to separate the sacred and the secular into their proper spheres perpetuate the tradition of Christendom the amendment was designed to end.[38]

TWO

THE FORMATION OF THE FIRST
AMENDMENT

 Americans frequently refer to the First Amendment as calling for
the "separation of Church and State." That term better describes
the struggle that preceded the enactment of the amendment, the struggle
that characterized the time following the legalization of Christianity,
the era of Christendom.

To describe modern America as separating Church and State is to
imply, at least, that Church and State had been united. Christendom
separated the sacred and the secular powers but assumed that both
would cooperate in upholding and promoting Christianity. Because
Christianity was deemed as an indispensable foundation of society, the
State promoted and protected it. An attack on Christianity was seen as
tantamount to treason and was treated as a capital offense. However,
despite the fact that secular and religious authorities agreed on the necessity of religion, they guarded fiercely their own powers and spheres
of authority. This determination on the part of each authority led to
endless conflicts between Church and State in the period between the
disintegration of the Roman Empire in the fifth century and the advent
of the Reformation in the sixteenth. Finding a method to define the
proper boundary between the two, or determining which was supreme,
proved impossible. At times, secular rulers attempted to control and
dominate the Church. At other times, religious leaders claimed supremacy in both Church and State.

In 1517, however, the Reformation begun by Martin Luther shattered
the unity of Western Catholic Christendom. Breaking with Rome and

Catholicism, most of Northern Europe followed Luther or other Protestant reformers. The long series of religious wars between Catholics and Protestants that lasted until 1648 exhausted the religious fervor of both. In an attempt to settle the Wars of Religion in Germany, both sides accepted, by way of the Peace of Augsburg in 1555, the principle *cuius regio, eius religio:* the religion of the ruler would determine the religion of the State. This compromise resolved—largely in favor of the secular power—the issue of the boundary between the secular and the sacred authorities that had continuously plagued Christendom.[1]

Puritanism

Within less than a century after the beginning of the Reformation, the spirit of revolt and religious fervor it had unleashed led to new religious divisions and wars. During the first half of the 1600s, England was engulfed in an enormous religious ferment known as Puritanism. Puritans held that the English monarchy had betrayed the Reformation by compromising with Catholicism, and they sought to reform Christianity by purifying it of Catholic remnants, particularly matters of ritual and ceremony. Some of them migrated to America to set up, in the wilderness of New England, what they believed would be a truly reformed Christendom. Their counterparts who remained in England engaged in a civil war in which they defeated and eventually executed their monarch, King Charles I. They then proceeded toward their goal of establishing a Christian commonwealth in that country.[2]

Religious Toleration

Having defeated their common enemy, the king, English Puritans began to disagree with each other over the nature of a true Christian commonwealth. The dream of unity and uniformity receded, and all parties eventually concluded that diversity of belief within the world of Protestantism had come to stay. In 1660, England returned to monarchy and the established Church of England, but Parliament subsequently recognized the fact of religious diversity in the Act of Toleration of 1689, which allowed Dissenters, (i.e., non-Anglican Protestants only) a bare toleration to practice their religion. The law still upheld and promoted an official church and deprived Dissenters—former Puritans for the most part—of many civil rights, including the right to hold government office. In the American colonies, to which it extended, the Act of Toleration brought about a high degree of religious harmony. Although many of the colonists were Dissenters from the Church of England, they did not experience the same deprivation of civil rights as did their coreligionists in the mother country.[3]

Religious Liberty

The same radical impulse that had motivated Puritans to challenge the manner in which the English government was implementing the Protestant Reformation prompted some of them to question whether government could carry out a religious reformation at all. They came to believe that only religious conviction and God's grace would produce the true Church and that government interference in religious matters would inevitably corrupt religion. To allow the secular power to exercise religious authority to select, determine, or enforce religious beliefs and practices would amount to surrendering the Church to the State. For religion to be truly authentic, it had to be freely exercised without government interference or coercion. In 1631, Roger Williams, a devoted Puritan, carried these ideas to America, and the concept of religious liberty took root in the New World.

Williams wanted above all to find and protect the true Church from the incursions and manipulations of the State. He loathed religious persecution, which he believed was anti-Christian, anti-Protestant, inhumane, and useless. For him, history proved that point: Catholics and Protestants had died equally heroically for their beliefs. Williams used what he referred to as the Two Tables of the Commandments to illustrate the legitimate power of government. Rulers could not involve themselves in matters pertaining to the First Table of the Commandments, those matters dealing with belief and worship. They could enforce only those Commandments belonging to the Second Table, which dealt with moral behavior.

Massachusetts authorities found Williams too extreme and banished him from that colony. He moved to Providence and became one of the founders of Rhode Island, a colony that provided religious liberty for all. It established no church, and it decreed that religion be supported voluntarily. In doing so, it abandoned the concept of Christendom, with the result that Rhode Island enjoyed a degree of religious liberty hitherto unknown to human experience. This extraordinary experiment little affected subsequent Church-State developments in America, however. In fact, taking their cue from Massachusetts, the other New England colonies joined in stigmatizing Rhode Island as a mismanaged settlement founded by irresponsible dissidents, and that reputation clung to it up to and through the American Revolution.[4]

In marked contrast to Rhode Island, Pennsylvania—founded by William Penn in 1682 as a "free colony" for all but especially for Quakers—provided an alternative to Christendom that exercised enormous influence on the growth of religious liberty in the American colonies. Quakers (initially a derogatory name for members of the Society of Friends) had arisen from within the Protestant tradition but had pushed the Reformation emphasis on the individual's relationship with God to its limits. They focused on the "inner light," a personal understanding guided by the spirit and grace of that relationship. Since they rejected religious organization and doctrinal correctness in favor of personal insight and inner direction, they felt no need to impose religious belief or practice on others. Thus, by its very nature, Quakerism was inimical to religious persecution.

Because they challenged and threatened both conventional religious behavior and existing religious organizations, Quakers drew persecution on themselves. By their emphasis on personal enlightenment rather than on Christian Scripture, they infuriated contemporary religious leaders—including Roger Williams. Consequently, they were heavily persecuted in both England and America—but never in Rhode Island.

Quakers accepted the same arguments Roger Williams and others in England and America had used in favor of religious liberty. However, they advanced that cause as much by example and practice as by argument. Whereas many of the outrageous persecutory acts committed by either Catholics or Protestants were recounted by those who would willingly have perpetrated similar atrocities against their oppressors, Quakers wanted nothing to do with persecuting others. They would not be silent, however, when they themselves were persecuted. Rather, with considerable skill, determination, and persistence, Quakers in America recorded and publicized punishments visited upon their members and reported them back to authorities in England, along with detailed accounts of taxes levied on them for the support of other churches. Thus did they bring to public discourse the understanding that persecution was cruel in and of itself, as well as anti-Christian and antihuman, thereby elevating the discussion of religious liberty to the level of humanitarianism.

Even more importantly for the cause of religious freedom, Pennsylvania Quakers demonstrated that a commonwealth that broke away from the practices of Christendom could not only survive, but also prosper. William Penn shared Roger Williams's horror of persecution for the sake of religion, as well as the latter's passion for true religion uncorrupted by civil authorities. But Penn's beliefs also included a strong pragmatic element. He was convinced not only that persecution destroyed true religion but that it was also bad for trade. Moreover, unlike Rhode Island, his colony could not be dismissed as populated by irresponsible dissidents. The sober citizens of Pennsylvania were subject to much legislation that in our time would be called "puritanical," including the prohibition of card playing, dice gaming, and stage plays.

Pennsylvania provided liberty of worship to all who believed in God and required that all religions be supported solely by means of voluntary offerings. (Quakers exhibited a particular loathing for paying religious tithes, believing that such taxes supported a purely human invention rather than a religion inspired by God.) Thus, William Penn had founded, for perhaps the first time in history, a large commonwealth that did not establish a church or a government-supported religion. The new colony of Pennsylvania not only survived, but it thrived and prospered. By the advent of the American Revolution, Philadelphia had become the most important city in the American colonies.

Under Quaker influence, nearby New Jersey and Delaware followed Pennsylvania's example. Moreover, Quakers carried their views on religious liberty and their deep aversion to tax-supported ministers and churches throughout the colonies. Such support would ultimately become a central issue in the many controversies regarding religious freedom that emerged in late colonial and revolutionary America.[5]

Beginning in the 1730s, the first colony-wide religious revival, the Great Awakening, swept through America. In its wake, a multitude of evangelical groups split from existing churches. These new religious communities frequently found themselves continuing to be taxed for the benefit of the "unreformed" churches they had left behind. In increasing numbers, they came to view the Pennsylvania experience as a model of true religious liberty, and to believe—like the Quakers—that voluntary support of religion was indispensable to its free exercise. Gradually, what had begun as resistance to taxation for a church other than one's own developed into widespread opposition to tax support for any religion.[6]

Religious Toleration and Religious Liberty

Of necessity, the distinction between religious toleration and religious liberty had to remain muted during the colonial period, inasmuch as religious toleration remained the standard of the empire of which the American colonies formed a part. Further, that same standard, according to which the English government upheld the toleration of minority Baptist and Quaker groups in New England, also ensured that colonies such as Pennsylvania could not exceed generally acceptable levels of religious toleration, for example, by allowing Catholics to participate in the political process.

Following the outbreak of the American Revolution, however, the differences between the traditions of religious toleration and religious liberty began to emerge in stark contrast. In the atmosphere of freedom the revolution engendered, the majority of the new states opted for religious liberty—abandoning established churches and requiring that religion be supported on a voluntary basis. Only Massachusetts, Connecticut, and New Hampshire continued the tradition of toleration beyond the revolutionary period. In settling on their individual Church- State arrangements, two of the new states, Virginia and Massachusetts, clearly demonstrated the dissimilarity between religious liberty and religious toleration.

Virginia: Religious Liberty and the End
of Christendom

During the colonial period, the Church of England had been established in Virginia. Its ministers and churches had been supported by a

tax on the colony's inhabitants. At the outbreak of the American Revolution, the new state of Virginia suspended these taxes but otherwise
left the structure of the established church intact. In drawing up a state
Bill of Rights, Virginians first proposed "full toleration of religion." At
the insistence of James Madison, however, its final version called for the
"free exercise" of religion.

After the revolution, Virginians again took up the topic of Church
and State. In the absence of public tax support, the formerly established
Anglican Church in the state was languishing, but a return to the former system of taxing everyone for its benefit was now out of the question. Instead, in 1784, Patrick Henry introduced a Bill to Enact a General Assessment for the support of all Christian churches that would
require all citizens to be taxed for the support of the church and minister of their choice. Those who wished to support no church or minister could opt to have their contributions go toward the support of education. Proponents of this bill defended it as promoting the general
welfare of society by strengthening morality and civic harmony. They
reasoned that such a general assessment would be compatible with religious liberty in that it allowed for no preference or preeminence among
churches, that is, no establishment of religion.

The proposed General Assessment Bill set off a chain of events that
produced one of the most important and decisive Church-State debates
ever to take place in America. James Madison launched the opposition
by publishing a petition known as *A Memorial and Remonstrance*. In
modern debate about the meaning of the First Amendment, this is virtually the only well-known petition. At the time, however, it ran a far
distant second to a much more popular petition submitted by many
counties and written from a more explicitly evangelical viewpoint than
that of Madison.[7]

Both petitions rejected Christendom, but the more popular one did
so in a more straightforward manner. Those petitioners pointed out that
Christianity had prospered when it was free from government power
and that its problems began only when Constantine first established it
by law. That development had led, in their estimation, to Christianity's
being overrun with "Error, Superstition, and Immorality." Lack of
state support, they insisted, would not lead to the triumph of Deism—
the eighteenth-century equivalent of modern secular humanism—as
supporters of the General Assessment Bill argued. Rather, true religion
would triumph, not by turning ministers into civil servants but by the

example and preaching of ministers motivated by faithfulness, piety, and the spirit of God. Pennsylvania, they noted, served as visible proof of the validity of their arguments.

These anti–General Assessment petitioners connected their belief in the welfare and interest of religion to the Enlightenment concept of "natural rights" as well. They declared that such an assessment would violate the guarantee of free exercise of religion, which to them meant voluntary exercise of religion, contained in Virginia's Bill of Rights. They demanded to be left "Intirely free in Matters of Religion and the manner of supporting its Ministers." The General Assessment Bill was swamped by the volume and intensity of opposition to it. In its stead, the Virginia legislature enacted Thomas Jefferson's *Bill for Establishing Religious Freedom,* which required that religion be supported entirely by voluntary contributions. With that, Virginians specifically rejected a system of Church and State that had persisted for almost fifteen centuries, thus proclaiming that, for them, Christendom had come to an end.

Massachusetts: Religious Toleration

For its part, Massachusetts chose to stay within the inherited tradition of toleration. In keeping with that tradition, the state government assumed the power to promote religion for the general welfare. In its constitution of 1780, Massachusetts declared that "the happiness of a people, and the good order and preservation of civil government, essentially depend upon piety, religion and morality," a statement the majority of Virginians would have agreed with entirely. However, Massachusetts went further and decided that morality and civility would disintegrate unless its government promoted religion. Therefore, its state constitution directed individual towns to make provision for public worship and the support of Protestant ministers. The latter were to be chosen by town majorities, and minorities could designate their taxes for the support of their own churches.[8]

When, as part of the ratification process, Massachusetts submitted the new constitution to the towns for discussion and approval, Article III for support of religion generated widespread and heated discussion. Opponents argued that such a provision injured religion by giving government power over it and that it violated liberty of conscience. They wanted no taxation at all for religion and believed, with the majority of

Virginians, that religion should be free of government power and should be supported voluntarily.[9]

Nevertheless, the majority of the state's towns supported Article III. Most citizens of Massachusetts equated religious liberty with the absence of government coercion but not with the absence of all government power to legislate in religious matters, and they held that their state maintained no establishment of religion in that it gave preference to no church. In fact, the provision for support of religion in its new constitution allowed Massachusetts to continue the long tradition of religious dominance by its Puritan founders and their Congregationalist successors. For two hundred years, by means of perseverance, ingenuity, and duplicity, they managed to maintain control of religion in the colony and subsequent state against pressure from without and dissent from within. All provisions for the support of religion in Massachusetts, including that of the Constitution of 1780, must be viewed in the context of that overall purpose.[10]

Massachusetts: A Historical Summary

Puritans had come to Massachusetts in 1630 to set up a Christian commonwealth, to build a true Protestant Christendom free from the Roman Catholic errors they saw being perpetuated in England. They had no tolerance for dissidents, and they said so plainly. As long as their Puritan allies governed England, they were able to sustain this policy of exclusion. In 1660, however, both the English monarchy and the established Church of England were restored, and Puritans in England and New England suddenly found themselves classified as Dissenters, subject—in England—to severe religious and civil disabilities. Despite this setback, Massachusetts Puritans, by then known as Congregationalists, determined to maintain their own preeminence in Church and State. Their majority status in the colony, as well as distance from England, aided them considerably in doing so.

Local control provided the key to continued Congregational superiority. The colonial Massachusetts government required each town to provide for a church and minister, and since Congregationalists controlled the towns, they also controlled the ecclesiastical system. In response to Anglican complaints sent to England that Massachusetts Dissenters were establishing their own religion, Congregationalists could argue that they were merely requiring the towns to provide for public worship of God and support of religion.

Congregationalists resisted every attack on their system. They kept the English Privy Council at bay and ignored or dismissed all opposition by non-Congregationalists in the colony. They made concessions only piecemeal and grudgingly. Under pressure from England, they did exempt Baptists and Quakers from religious taxation, but made all requests for such exemptions subject to approval by local Congregationalist majorities. Baptists, in particular, continued to suffer petty harassment, social condescension, and what they regarded as religious persecution.

Congregationalists' determination to maintain their own dominance in the colony and subsequent state is the vital factor in understanding Church-State relations in Massachusetts. Their arguments all served that ulterior purpose and were therefore intended to equivocate and to obfuscate rather than to clarify. During the colonial era, their protestations were designed to shield them from accusations by the English government that they, as Dissenters, had in fact established their own Church in derogation of the Church of England.[11] After the revolution, in the era of liberty, when many complained that the old oppression was still in effect, defenders of the Massachusetts Church-State system proclaimed that it was perfectly compatible with freedom, in that it preferred no church and imposed no doctrine. For two centuries, Massachusetts Puritans and their Congregationalist successors maintained their domination, in spite of outside influence and internal opposition. Not until 1833, after Congregationalists themselves had split into Trinitarians and Unitarians, did the system collapse.[12]

Religious Toleration and Religious Liberty Contrasted

In direct contrast to Virginia and much of the rest of America, Massachusetts defined religious liberty in negative terms—as the Supreme Court would later define it—as the absence of government coercion or restraint of religious practice or belief. According to this definition, government could promote religious belief as long as it did not force anyone to accept it. Proponents of state support for religion at the time argued that such was perfectly compatible with freedom of religion.

Opponents of it in Massachusetts knew well from experience that the system was in reality intended to support Congregationalist dominance. The Massachusetts Constitution of 1780 forced them to conform to the Congregationalist viewpoint and required them to pay taxes for the support of religion, even though they believed such a system violated religious liberty and conferred unlawful power upon the government.

Those who upheld the Massachusetts system took a pessimistic approach to religion and society. They thought of religion in utilitarian terms, as morality ensuring social control. The politically radical Congregationalist ministers in New England, whose salaries were paid at public expense, adhered to that perspective. They had long ago abandoned the dream of bringing about a true Christian commonwealth, and instead had come to see religion in terms of a system of ethical values that could be employed for the common good.

By contrast, Evangelicals throughout the states, who opposed tax support for religion, believed in the transforming power of conversion, grace, and the spirit. They were convinced that religion, freely exercised and removed from government control, would produce the kind of religious conviction needed to sustain a virtuous society; whereas government interference in religion would kill the spirit and produce only a deadening conformity.

Modern Understanding of the Historical Background of the First Amendment

Until 1947, cases dealing with religious issues that had come before the Supreme Court consisted, for the most part, of claims by individuals of government coercion of their religious beliefs. The Court had traditionally dealt with these as involving the Free Exercise provision of the First Amendment. Thus, it had come to equate Free Exercise with the absence of government coercion of religious beliefs or practice rather than with religion freely and voluntarily practiced without any government meddling, well motivated or not.

In 1947, however, the Court addressed itself to a new issue— whether a state could reimburse parents for the cost of transporting their children to parochial schools. This case did not involve a claim of

coercion, and the Court decided that the matter fell within the purview
of No Establishment. Accordingly, it addressed itself to the meaning of
that provision and of the First Amendment in general. The Court's decision in this case created the format for the modern debate over the
historical meaning of the amendment. Although the decision immediately generated passionate supporters and opponents, members of both
groups accepted its framework and presuppositions as the basis for their
arguments.

In a later case, Justice Hugo Black concisely explained as follows the
principal premise underlying the Court's approach to the meaning of
the First Amendment:

> Although these two clauses may in certain instances overlap, they forbid
> two quite different kinds of governmental encroachment upon religious
> freedom. The Establishment Clause, unlike the Free Exercise Clause,
> does not depend upon any showing of direct governmental compulsion
> and is violated by the enactment of laws which establish an official reli-
> gion whether those laws operate directly to coerce nonobserving indi-
> viduals or not.[13]

In this fateful, profoundly erroneous assumption, the Court missed entirely the development of religious liberty from Roger Williams,
through William Penn's Pennsylvania experiment, and through the
Virginia of the 1780s. It settled instead on the Massachusetts notion
that the free exercise of religion meant no more than toleration and the
absence of government coercion. It failed to grasp that religious liberty
involved the concept of natural rights, that free exercise of religion
equated with freedom from government control or interference altogether apart from specific oppression of believers, and that it had come
to be understood as synonymous with voluntary exercise of religion.

By thus equating Free Exercise with toleration, that is, with a government benefit to individuals, the Supreme Court not only misunder-
stood the true historical meaning of religious freedom but failed to
comprehend the original purpose of the First Amendment. According
to the Court's definition, if the Framers had omitted the No Establishment provision and relied, as Virginia did, only on Free Exercise, the
federal government would have had power to establish a religion, provided it coerced no one. However, the original purpose of the amendment was to make explicit the fact that the federal government had no
power at all over religious belief, practice, or devotion.

The result of this failure to understand the historical development of religious freedom and the free exercise of religion has been that modern discussion about government sponsorship of—and exercise of power in—religion is carried out under the heading of establishment of religion. This reality has placed an insuperable burden on the No Establishment provision in that it has forced critics and supporters of the Supreme Court's 1947 approach into trying to find meanings for "establishment of religion" that never existed. During the era preceding the enactment of the First Amendment, the concept of the free exercise of religion had developed dramatically, while the understanding of establishment of religion never changed. Present-day Church-State discussion and scholarship have reversed this history.

That so many American scholars and jurists could have adopted the historical misassumptions of the Court and built a huge structure of scholarship so out of harmony with historical evidence is itself a phenomenon of modern history. Following the 1947 decision, proponents and opponents of the Court's interpretation were able to devise historical arguments that seemed to provide their members with decisive evidence for the correctness of their positions. In ensuing years, however, both groups have been able to adhere to their respective certainties only by ignoring massive amounts of countervailing evidence and by engaging in determined historical selectivity. The historical evidence they have focused on falls into three categories. The first of these involves the contemporary definition of establishment of religion at the time of the enactment of the First Amendment. The second entails the assertion that, particularly by way of the Massachusetts and other New England Church-State systems, Americans at the time experienced non-preferential government sponsorship of religion. The third centers on the belief that in the course of the General Assessment controversy, Virginians debated and clarified the meaning of an establishment of religion.

The Understanding of Establishment
of Religion in 1789

In 1789, the House of Representatives of the First Congress sent to the Senate the following proposed amendment regarding religion: "Congress shall make no law establishing religion, or prohibiting the free exercise thereof, nor shall the rights of conscience be infringed." The

Senate wanted different wording. First, some senators proposed that "Congress shall make no law establishing one religious sect or society in preference to others." After more debate, however, the majority of the Senate settled for "Congress shall make no law establishing articles of faith or a mode of worship, or prohibiting the free exercise of religion." The House, however, declined this version, and a joint committee settled on the present wording: "Congress shall make no law respecting an establishment of religion, or prohibiting the free exercise thereof." In the modern debate about the meaning of the First Amendment, the difference between the Senate versions and the final formulation settled on by the joint committee is crucial.

On the basis of logical analysis alone, modern scholars and commentators have read into the formats advanced by the senators a proof that members of Congress clashed over diverse meanings of the term "establishment of religion." If, as the modern argument holds, Congress had prohibited only the imposition of "articles of faith or a mode of worship," or only the establishment of any one religion in preference to others, the First Amendment would have been essentially different from the one we have. Both sides agree it would have granted the government power in religious matters, provided it preferred no one religion or imposed no beliefs on the populace. One party to the modern debate argues that the House appreciated that danger and demanded an amendment prohibiting any law "respecting an establishment" of religion. Opponents maintain—with good historical evidence to back them—that Americans at the time universally understood an establishment of religion to mean a government preference for one church, sect, or religion. Therefore, they assert that the First Amendment did not prohibit government sponsorship on an equitable basis of all religions or religion in general. [14]

Neither side can produce a single piece of historical evidence to prove that members of the First Congress clashed over the meaning of an establishment of religion. No history from the time warrants the belief that Americans adhered to different definitions of an establishment of religion, and all the available evidence supports the belief that they did not.[15]

To hold that government did or can assist all religions on a nonpreferential basis is to ignore a fundamental assumption that undergirded the formation of the federal government. James Madison saw religion as a source of faction. He believed that a tendency to form factions around religious belief was part of human nature and that freedom would be protected by way of mutually suspicious religious groups checking and balancing each other. To give the government power in religious matters would inevitably lead to a struggle for dominance on the part of one or a number of factions. To suppose that government could promote, on an equitable basis, religious groups different from—or even repugnant to—the majority of those in power is to make assumptions altogether at variance with his thought.

Historical evidence that Americans in 1789 universally defined establishment of religion as a government preference for one religion is certain and unambiguous. When Madison introduced a Bill of Rights, he explained that he wanted to forestall a "national religion," one that might obtain preeminence and to which others would be obliged to conform. John Leland, a Baptist minister and one of the leaders of the movement for a Bill of Rights, also thought of establishment in terms of preference. People in the states that stayed with the tradition of tolerance as well as those that progressed to religious liberty all thought similarly about establishment. Massachusetts decreed that "no subordination of any one denomination to another shall ever be established by law." Pennsylvania, whose tradition differed diametrically from that of Massachusetts, similarly required that "no preference shall ever be given by law to any religious establishments or modes of worship."[16]

Americans' common agreement on the definition of establishment of religion proceeded from their history and experience. In their minds, two churches above all exemplified establishment of religion. The first of these was the Roman Catholic Church, going back to Constantine. The second, with which they were more immediately familiar, was the established Church of England, which John Adams described as "creeds, articles, tests, ceremonies, and tithes." In the 1760s, a petition by some Anglican clergy for the appointment of bishops to the colonies united Americans throughout the colonies in a frenzy of opposition. They believed that the appointment of bishops would carry the English Anglican establishment to America.[17] They knew that establishment always involved a government preference. The logical inference drawn by modern scholars—that those who wanted to prohibit the establishment of any one religion thereby implied that government could assist all religions—would have astonished them.

When the senators proposed different wordings for the First Amendment, they were employing the common usage of the time and imitating the phrasing of state constitutions. We have no evidence for why the House rejected the final Senate wording, but we can be sure that it was not because of a substantive difference. Thomas Jefferson, who certainly did not approve of any power on the part of government in religious matters, echoed the Senate wordings when he later drew up a Bill of Rights for the new state of Kentucky, wherein he wrote that "no preference shall ever be given by law to any religious societies or modes of worship."[18]

Much of the discussion of the meaning of establishment of religion in 1789 has focused on a textual analysis of phrases from the *Annals of Congress,* isolated from and in conflict with the very considerable contemporary body of evidence about the meaning of that term. Literalism, which has so influenced modern American religion, has also penetrated the historical and legal professions. Drawing abstract conclusions from texts without attempting to corroborate those conclusions with historical evidence or without accounting for the motivation of the historical participants prevents scholars from appreciating the accomplishments of the past. It sacrifices experience and history to logic.

The Massachusetts Church-State System

To sustain the abstract logical position that when Americans in 1789 banned the establishment of any one church in preference to others they implied consent for nonpreferential government assistance to all churches, participants in the modern debate have had to create imaginary historical scenarios. Massachusetts and Connecticut merely appeared to demonstrate that Americans were aware of nonpreferential government power in religion.

During the colonial era, Massachusetts Congregationalists hid their religious dominance under the guise of local control, and they continued to do so after the American Revolution. To all dissent, they answered that their system violated no one's liberty, since it coerced no one and established no religion because no one church or group was preferred. Non-Congregationalists knew from experience, however, that the system was imposed by a majority for its own benefit. In 1769, Baptists even formed a Grievance Committee to protest their mistreatment and religious inequality.[19]

Isaac Backus, a Baptist minister and a representative of the Baptists in their struggles for religious liberty, spent his life fighting the New England Church-State arrangements. In criticizing the Massachusetts system for the support of religion, he pleaded, as have all oppressed groups in response to the rationalization and callousness of majorities, to "let them only change places with us." Backus and those others who, during the debate in the Massachusetts towns on the Constitution of 1780 opposed government support to religion, perceived the proposed system as inherently preferential. They did not seek a change in the definition of an establishment of religion; they simply wanted the state to live up to the one it had enacted. Opponents of government-sponsored religion knew from history and experience that establishment always involved preference. They knew that the system they lived under was not nonpreferential, as surely as later generations would know that "separate but equal" racial systems were not equal. It is a tribute to the effectiveness of the New England Congregationalists that the stratagems they devised to mask their own dominance continue to mislead modern scholars.

The Virginia General Assessment and Nonpreferential Establishment

In interpreting the historical meaning of No Establishment, the Supreme Court relied above all on the experience of Virginia during the 1780s, the decade in which that state decisively rejected a General Assessment Bill designed to provide public support for multiple Christian groups. James Madison led the fight against it, and he later shepherded the Bill of Rights through the First Congress. These actions would appear to provide decisive evidence that Madison and the majority of Virginians understood and rejected an establishment of religion more inclusive than a state preference for a single church.

The fundamental problem with connecting the Virginia experience with No Establishment, however, is that the General Assessment controversy had nothing at all to do with clarifying the meaning of an establishment of religion. Neither the General Assessment Bill itself nor Thomas Jefferson's *Bill for Religious Liberty* that was enacted in its stead referred to establishment of religion. Virginia had no law prohibiting an establishment, and its citizens indicated no need for such a statute.

They dealt with the matter of a general assessment in terms of the free exercise of religion guaranteed them by Virginia's Bill of Rights.[20]

Surely, however, the General Assessment Bill proposed a broad non-preferential support for religion. After all, such supporters as George Washington considered the proposal fair and reasonable. At a distance of more than two hundred years and from a modern isolated perspective, this may still seem to be the case. But that was not how contemporary opponents saw it. For them, the General Assessment controversy represented a major battle in their long struggle to overthrow the preeminence of the formerly established Anglican Church in Virginia and bring religious equality to the state. This campaign did not end until 1802, when the state confiscated the glebes—public lands granted to the Anglican Church during the colonial period.[21]

Baptist ministers in Virginia were still enduring persecution and imprisonment for preaching on the eve of the American Revolution. Even after the war's outbreak, Anglican petitioners informed the Virginia legislature of their alarm at the progress of some of the "Dissenters from the Church by Law Established," who were "inducing the ignorant and unwary to embrace their erroneous Tenets." They asked that these groups be properly restricted by state law.[22] Moreover, after the war ended, non-Anglicans continued to suffer social and religious disabilities.

Local government in Virginia remained dominated by vestries, which were limited to members of the Anglican Church. Non-Anglicans had to pay Anglican clergymen to perform weddings and funerals. In 1780, the state legislature did license non-Anglican ministers to perform marriages, but they continued to experience restrictions that Anglican ministers did not. Those who fought the General Assessment Bill were convinced that the Anglican Church retained special privileges and that the assessment proposal had been designed solely for the purpose of maintaining and extending those distinctions.

In 1784, the Anglican Church in Virginia secured an Act of Incorporation from the state, a development that greatly alarmed non-Anglicans, who saw it as another step on the road to reestablishment of the Anglican—now Episcopal—Church. The Presbyterian ministers of the state, in petitioning the Assembly, lamented the continuing "evident predilection" for the Anglican Church and the "partiality which we are sorry to have observed so long." Following the defeat of the

General Assessment Bill, however, non-Anglicans also brought about the repeal of the Act of Incorporation.[23]

Only by abstracting the General Assessment Bill from its historical context can modern commentators find in it a proposal for nonpreferential support. To the majority of Virginians at the time, it was anything but nonpreferential. They knew it to be essentially an attempt to rescue the formerly established Church, which had lost its state support and was languishing under a voluntary system. They viewed it as an attempt to use the power of the state to benefit one religious group. This attitude on their part explains why they never altered their definition of establishment as preferential. It also explains why James Madison, who so opposed the bill, could refer to Virginia as having no "exclusive establishment" and continue to think of establishment solely in terms of a preference for one religion.

The Argument from Federalism

In recent years, an assertion that the No Establishment provision of the First Amendment was added to protect existing state establishments of religion from federal interference, that it was an "exercise in federalism," has gained popularity.[24] This argument relies heavily on an assumption that the states maintained establishments of religion. However, by the time the amendment was enacted into law, there were no official state establishments in America.[25] Rhode Island, Pennsylvania, New Jersey, and Delaware had never established a religion. New York, the Carolinas, and Virginia had abandoned the establishments they had inherited. Maryland allowed for a general assessment type of support, of the kind that Virginia had proposed, but the majority of the people of the state decisively defeated its implementation. Georgia provided for a similar arrangement, but this was apparently never implemented either. Massachusetts, Connecticut, and New Hampshire did not legislate establishments of religion, and the supporters of the Church-State systems there would have vigorously denied that they constituted an establishment of religion.[26] The First Amendment was not intended to protect the establishments in the states because in the understanding of Americans at the time, there were no state establishments to protect.

Apart from the fact that the supposed beneficiaries of this "exercise in federalism" did not see themselves as supporting establishments of religion, the weakness of the argument is exposed by the reality that the states that should have been most concerned showed little interest in an amendment limiting the jurisdiction of the federal government in religious matters by way of the First Amendment. Two presumed beneficiaries, Massachusetts and Connecticut, manifested no interest in an amendment regarding religion. They neither proposed an amendment dealing with establishment nor ratified the First Amendment at the time.[27] Supporters of state authority in religious matters knew that as far as religion was concerned, the Constitution itself was an exercise in federalism. They knew, as well as did Madison and Hamilton, that the federal government possessed no authority in religious matters.[28]

In the course of the House debate, Congressman Huntington of Connecticut did express a fear that the amendment prohibiting an establishment of religion might be construed in such a way as to negate the New England tax arrangements for the support of ministers and churches. Typical of New England Congregationalists, he refrained from describing his state's system as an establishment but worried that the federal courts might construe it as such. However, no evidence indicates that any other New Englanders shared his concern. On the contrary, in the same debate, Roger Sherman, also from Connecticut, and who had attended the Constitutional Convention, pointed out that an amendment was quite unnecessary since the federal government was without power in religious matters. Given the lack of interest on the part of Connecticut and Massachusetts in either proposing or ratifying any amendment regarding religion, Sherman clearly represented the prevailing beliefs in those states.[29]

The desire for an amendment protecting religious liberty from interference by government came from those most concerned with protecting the rights of conscience. They had no desire to bestow power over religious matters upon the states. [30] Rather, they wanted to be sure that the new government would not assume powers they had never given to—or had already taken away from—the states.[31]

One of the difficulties with the "exercise in federalism" argument is that it depreciates the extraordinary American achievement of religious liberty by focusing on what the states did not do rather than on what they did. Adherents of this point of view focus not on the revolution that America brought about in Church and State but on the remnants of Christendom that perdured. Evaluating the history preceding and surrounding the First Amendment in terms of the vague and indefinable term of "separation" or projecting back into the past "multiple" or "plural" establishments of religion—terms unknown at the time—only promotes a misunderstanding of that history.[32] The great majority of states, in fact, had either never set up any establishment of religion or had dismantled the establishments they had inherited from prerevolutionary times. In the estimation of their citizens, they had abandoned Christendom and inaugurated complete religious liberty. While they did not implement that principle in every aspect of Church and State, their accomplishments on its behalf were enormous, fundamental, and enduring.

Because the preponderance of the population participated in a common culture and shared a common Protestantism, few Americans were motivated to challenge cultural religious practices that in fact perpetuated elements of Christendom by involving states in the exercise of power in religious matters. Some practices, such as Sunday legislation, or laws to protect the integrity of the Bible, were considered to represent the norm of civilized living. Others, such as the persistence of laws excluding Catholics and non-Christians from voting rights, represented the persistence of habits and attitudes still in the process of change.[33] Americans in most of the states certainly did not view these practices in terms of a coherent Church-State system as did the defenders of the religious systems in Massachusetts and Connecticut. Thus, they did not conceive of the First Amendment as enacted to protect state ecclesiastical systems. As chapter 3 will explain, immigrant Catholics would become the catalyst of a new awareness and understanding that observances and practices accepted by the majority of Americans were coercive, oppressive, and religiously preferential.

The problem with the argument that the First Amendment was enacted to protect existing state establishments of religion is that it lacks sustaining historical evidence. The pity of the argument is that it obscures one of the great advances in Western civilization. The ideas put forth so passionately by Roger Williams and so prudently by William Penn lit fires of enlightenment in thousands of colonial minds. They inspired the conviction that religious belief would be true and vibrant only if it were free and voluntary. A majority of Americans came to believe that for government to withdraw from religious affairs would be good for both Church and State. To reduce this movement, one that broke with the practice of a millennium-and-a-half of Christendom, to a scheme to protect the dying remnants of the petty tyrannical New England Church-State systems represents a lamentable loss of historical wisdom.

Summary

In 1789, the people of the United States demanded a specific assurance that the new federal government would have limited and specified powers and that it would not threaten religious liberty. With the enactment of the First Amendment, they acknowledged the end of the long tradition of Christendom, in which government had exercised power to uphold, promote, and support religion. The amendment addressed itself to government only. It was intended to free religion from state power and interference and allow it to prosper or not, according to the conviction of religious believers. Many of them believed that the exercise of religion free from government manipulation and interference would unleash the spirit and that religion would prosper in America as never before. Subsequent history appears to have validated many of their hopes.

Because modern scholars, jurists, and historians have forgotten this original purpose, they have devised arguments utterly at odds with historical evidence. On the one hand, they have returned to the habit of attempting to draw proper boundaries between the secular and the sacred, between Church and State. Instead of focusing on what is secular, what properly belongs within the government's realm, they have concentrated on what is religious, what helps or hinders religion. Instead of asking how a law affects the state, whether it exceeds the powers delegated to government, they look to how it affects religion. This focus leads government officials and judges back to deciding what is "essentially religious," something forbidden to them by the First Amendment.

Thus, the modern approach to the First Amendment has resulted in the creation of a spurious conflict. On the one hand, government sees itself as promoting Free Exercise. On the other, it sees itself as forbidden by No Establishment to aid religion. The problem this interpretation poses for modern judges is: How can government promote Free Exercise without running afoul of No Establishment?

The fallacy of the modern approach is the assumption that religious liberty is the gift of government and that prohibition of an establishment equates with prohibition of government aid to religion. In reality, the First Amendment is an acknowledgment that the people are already free in the exercise of religion and that the government will not interfere with that freedom by attempting to wield power in it or to make decisions about it. The amendment fulfills the unitary purpose of declaring that government has no power in religion and "shall make no law" pretending to authority in it. The proclamation of Free Exercise represented the great development in human liberty that had occurred in American history, while No Establishment signified and specified the abandonment of the traditional approach to religion and government that great development represented.

To argue that government can exercise power in religion on a non-preferential basis is not only to misunderstand the First Amendment but also to misinterpret human experience, history, the nature of religion, and the view of human nature that helped generate the amendment. Free exercise of religion meant voluntarily exercised religion, liberated from all attempts to legislate or enforce religious beliefs, practices, or requirements. Prohibition of an establishment of religion meant that government should not select, promote, or prefer one religious group, a practice familiar to many Americans at the time the First Amendment was enacted. America defined the role of the State; it left the Church free to define its own role and what was good or bad for religion. It abandoned Christendom and with it the historical search for a proper dividing line between Church and State.

THREE

THE CONTINUING EMERGENCE
OF RELIGIOUS LIBERTY

The year 1789, in which Congress enacted the Bill of Rights, also marked the start of the French Revolution. Both events would entail momentous implications for Church and State in America and in France since both proclaimed the end of Christendom. This one common result, however, exhausted the similarities between the two countries in their approach to religion. Whereas Americans forbade their new government to exercise power in religious matters, the French endowed their new state with power over the Church. Revolutionary Americans believed that the free exercise of religion would nurture the virtue needed to maintain a republican form of government. For revolutionaries in France, religion came to be seen as the mortal enemy of the Republic. For Americans today, the contrast between those actions and attitudes of two centuries ago is particularly significant because both the imagery used and the justification for some Church–State decisions advanced in this country derive more from the French than from the American historical experience.

The French Revolution and Religion

In its initial phase, the French Revolution attempted to make religion a department of the State. By depriving the Catholic Church of its property, the French National Assembly rendered it dependent upon govern-

46

ment support. The Civil Constitution of the Clergy, enacted in 1790, reorganized the Catholic Church in France and turned the clergy into paid civil servants. Religion would serve a social, cultural, and political function, as it had in the Roman Empire before the reign of Constantine. However, this redesign of the Church succeeded only in turning a large body of French Catholics against the revolution. Henceforth, conflict between supporters of the Church and Monarchy on one side, and adherents of the Revolution and Republic on the other polarized the French nation.

Having failed to make religion the servant of the state, the French revolutionaries moved to the more radical position of eliminating it altogether. If Christianity could not be controlled, then it had to be replaced with an ideology more compatible with the political beliefs of the revolution. Accordingly, the revolutionaries set out to systematically dismantle the culture that had evolved during the era of Christendom in France. It designated 1792, the first year of the Republic, as Year One. It recast the calendar to eliminate the Christian Sabbath. It devised its own form of religion, as exemplified by the ceremonies conducted in the Cathedral of Notre Dame, itself renamed the Temple of Reason.

These two impulses—to control religion and render it a tool of the state or to eliminate it altogether—would continue to dominate Church-State relations in France. Both served to augment the power of the State in religious matters. Thus, religious liberty never became the focus of the French Revolution. Rather, that revolution attempted to draw boundaries between Church and State in such a way as to circumscribe and confine religion so that it would be incapable of competing with the ideology of the revolution. As a result, France became a battleground of warring beliefs and the State a prize to be captured either by the forces of revolution or those of the counterrevolution.[1]

French Revolutionary Imagery and America

The image of the *wall of separation* between Church and State, which has figured so prominently in modern American Church-State discussion, better suggests the approach of the French Revolution than that reflected by the American Constitution and the First Amendment. In

1947, Justice Hugo Black, writing for the majority of the Supreme Court, ignited the modern Church–State debate in a decision that included the following much-quoted paragraph:

> The "establishment of religion" clause of the First Amendment means at least this: Neither a state nor the Federal Government can set up a church. Neither can pass laws which aid one religion, aid all religions, or prefer one religion over another. Neither can force nor influence a person to go to or to remain away from church against his will or force him to profess a belief or disbelief in any religion. No person can be punished for entertaining or professing religious beliefs or disbeliefs, for church attendance or non-attendance. No tax in any amount, large or small, can be levied to support any religious activities or institutions, whatever they may be called, or whatever form they may adopt to teach or practice religion. Neither a state nor the Federal Government can, openly or secretly, participate in the affairs of any religious organizations or groups and *vice versa*. In the words of Jefferson, the clause against establishment of religion by law was intended to erect "a wall of separation between Church and State."[2]

In his years as a member of the Supreme Court, from 1937 to 1971, Justice Black limited himself to treasuring and protecting the exact words of the Constitution to such an extent that he made sure to have a copy of the text constantly with him. It is an irony of modern Church–State relations that one so devoted to the actual text of the Constitution is largely responsible for obscuring the wording of the First Amendment by replacing it with a metaphorical expression. The metaphor of the *wall of separation* popularized by Justice Black had been coined by Thomas Jefferson in 1802 in a reply to an address sent him by the Baptists in Danbury, Connecticut. In that response, Jefferson had maintained the integrity of American thinking on Church and State by citing in full the section on religion from the First Amendment, by describing religion as a voluntary activity, and by specifying the limited power of government. Almost 150 years later, however, the Court appropriated his *wall of separation* metaphor and enshrined it as the preeminent image of Church and State in America.[3]

No one has ever been able to define the *wall*. Nevertheless, for many of those who followed the Court's interpretation as represented in Justice Black's opinion, defending it took on the aura of a crusade. The image also captured the Court's critics, who found themselves discussing legal matters in the same metaphorical terms, in that they argued that the *wall* had never existed at all.

Apart altogether from the *wall* metaphor, Justice Black read into the First Amendment a series of meanings completely at odds with its history. Ensuing acceptance of this paragraph as a topic of debate has made it impossible to correlate Church-State jurisprudence with the history of the amendment.

The understanding that No Establishment has to do with aid to religion has been one of the crucial misassumptions on the part of the Supreme Court about the purpose of the First Amendment. The justices all accepted this understanding, but they divided on its application to the case at hand, which concerned reimbursement of parents for the transportation of their children to parochial schools.

Justice Black's majority opinion approved such reimbursement, but four dissenting justices excoriated the majority for doing so, given the definition of Establishment they, too, had just agreed upon. They vehemently insisted that such reimbursement amounted to aid to religion, something the majority opinion had forbidden. Their intensity, however, can be viewed as straining at gnats while swallowing a camel. The dissenting justices quarreled over the pittance involved in New Jersey's transporting children to parochial schools, but they unhesitatingly accepted the fact that the same state sanctioned the education provided by those schools. By thus accepting parochial school education as fulfilling a public purpose, states throughout the country aided, to an incalculable degree, Catholicism and other religions that maintained religious schools.

The decision to accept religious schools as fulfilling a public purpose, thus aiding the churches that conducted those schools, had been made in 1925 in response to an attempt by the state of Oregon to force all children to attend public schools.[4] For Catholics particularly and for some other religions, parochial or religious schools have played a crucial role in their missions. This could never have happened if states had not assisted by recognizing these schools as fulfilling a public purpose. The immense aid to religion that ensued from this policy on the part of state governments serves to highlight the discontinuity between the Court's decisions and its rhetoric.

Those countries that followed the ideological tradition of the French Revolution and wanted "a complete and permanent separation of the spheres of religious activity and civil authority" sought to isolate religion and deny it any possible aid. Consequently, in those countries, religious schools became the flash point in the struggle between religion and revolutionary ideology for the hearts and minds of the people. Fortunately, the Supreme Court in practice has followed Jefferson's understanding that the First Amendment requires the government to deal with action only, not belief. The amendment is not about government aid to religion because the government has no power to define religion, let alone what aids it.

Believers in the *wall* raised the cry "No aid!" when they should have proclaimed "No power!" In American history, many of the most fervent supporters of the First Amendment believed passionately—and correctly—that the amendment would be of enormous aid to true religion. The First Amendment is a limitation on government only. It declares where the power of the State, not the Church, ends. It is not designed to give government authority to deal with the essentially religious question of what aids churches or to wield the enormous power that would be required to create two entirely separate spheres of human activity. The *wall of separation* metaphor represents the French preoccupation with controlling the power of religion, not the American one with controlling the power of government.

In its focus on the *wall* metaphor, the Court returned to the preoccupation of Christendom with defining the limits of the secular and the sacred. Americans had solved this historic problem of Christendom by avoiding it. The Constitution defined the limits of the State, but left the churches free to define their own limits.

Thomas Jefferson is remembered for his metaphor of the *wall*. When, as president, he refused to appoint days of thanksgiving and fasting, he explained that "no power to prescribe any religious exercises or to assume authority in religious discipline, has been delegated to the General Government." The president had been entrusted with "civil powers alone." Had the Supreme Court in 1947 chosen to focus on this lucid and accurate description of the First Amendment, it would thereby have avoided much subsequent confusion.[5]

In his much-quoted paragraph cited above, Justice Black moved on to the subject of prohibiting any tax to support religious activities. This sweeping statement contradicted the realities of American life and what the Court itself had protected. It provided another source of the confusion that has engulfed modern discussion of the First Amendment, the purpose of which was to prevent government from legislating religious activities. However, the Court has translated this prohibition into a permission to examine the religious consequences of secular legislation. If followed in practice, this approach would make the Court all powerful by conferring on it authority to examine all laws using a religious criterion, namely, whether they aided or hindered religion.

Many laws have an impact on religion. Tax exemption statutes include nonprofit religious groups and assist religion. The exercise of the right upheld by the Court itself to use public parks for religious gatherings often involves expenditure of public tax funds for police protection and crowd control. Without such expenditures, many such events for the propagation of religion could not occur. Government may employ individuals or organizations to perform secular tasks, such as caring for the poor, homeless, or refugees. Those performing these tasks may endow them with profound religious significance and may be motivated primarily by religious fervor. However, these religious ramifications of secular projects are not for the Court to investigate or determine.

Further, according to Justice Black's definition of it, the *wall* proscribes government participation in the affairs of religious organizations and vice versa. On the basis of common experience, this statement is manifestly wrong. Governments habitually participate and interfere in the affairs of churches by enforcing zoning restrictions, building and safety regulations, and other codes. For tax purposes, they distinguish between different types of church properties. In internal church property conflicts, courts will rule on ownership of the contested property.

In its "vice versa" reference—participation of churches in the affairs of government—the statement is even more obviously incorrect. Throughout American history, churches and religious groups have been active in a wide range of political issues, such as antislavery movements, civil rights, immigration matters, war and peace, and capital punishment. Here again, the Court has not followed the logic of its rhetoric. Rather, it has upheld the right of religious groups to involve themselves in such political matters. It has even upheld the right of ministers of religion to run for political office.[6]

Critics of the Court and Their Use of History

Those who oppose the Supreme Court's 1947 decision on the meaning of the First Amendment also rely on history to provide a different interpretation of it. However, their approach to the historical evidence has been as flawed as that of the Court and its defenders. They insist that continuing involvement in religious matters by both federal and state governments clearly demonstrates that the amendment did not create a *wall of separation* between Church and State. For example, the very Congress that enacted it appointed chaplains to both House and Senate, as well as to the armed forces, and issued a proclamation calling for a religious day of thanksgiving. Individual states acted similarly. They passed Sabbath laws, mandated prayer and Bible reading in the schools, and upheld the ethos, beliefs, and practices of Protestant Christianity in a multitude of ways.[7]

Critics of the Court contend that the founding generation surely understood what was meant by religious liberty, and its practices thus should be taken as normative. This argument, when advanced—as it usually is—apart from its historical context, leads to several conclusions that are at odds with the historical development of the United States.

First, it is a mistake to assume that all historical examples exemplify contemporary principles. Few principles espoused during the American Revolution could pass that test. Although Americans enacted the Constitution and the Bill of Rights, they nevertheless continued, and even strengthened, practices that were at odds with liberty, equality, and government by the people. Not everything they did promoted the general welfare or secured to all the blessings of liberty. Indeed, much that they did fell short of their stated principles, including that of religious liberty.

Second, to evaluate the implementation of American principles according to a standard of logical consistency rather than according to the experience of those who enunciated them is to misinterpret American history. Although Americans, in adopting the First Amendment, rejected Christendom, they did not—like the French revolutionaries—set out to systematically dismantle every manifestation of that system and devise a completely new code of human behavior. Instead, they implemented their principles by way of specific and immediate controversies and in the absence of conflict, tended to revert to traditional and familiar practice.

The continued sponsorship of religion by government at all levels is not a guide to the original meaning of the First Amendment but an illustration of how far America had yet to progress in order to implement its stated principle of religious liberty. For most contemporary Americans, the amendment represented the definite end of a process. With the dismantling of existing Church-State systems—New England excepted—and the implementation of a voluntary system of support for churches, they considered the matter of religious liberty settled. Indeed, for the great majority, the pinnacle of religious freedom had been reached.

In some matters, Americans could at least dimly perceive the future unfolding of their fundamental principles. For example, a nation whose Constitution referred to African-American slaves as "other" could at least intuit that its declaration of the created equality of all had still not been fully implemented. Such was not the case with religious freedom, however. Once the final major divisive religious issue, support of churches and ministers, had been resolved, Americans experienced extensive religious harmony. Their common Protestantism created a unity that transcended the boundaries of their individual churches. This lack of divisiveness contributed in part to what became known as the Era of Good Feeling. The homogeneity John Jay had celebrated in the *Federalist Papers*—"a people descended from the same ancestors, speaking the same language, professing the same religion, attached to the same principles of government, very similar in their manners and customs"—became even more manifest.[8] In the absence of other significant religious-cultural groups, they came to think of their world as the entire world and of their experience of religious liberty as normative for all times and places. They believed that America provided complete religious freedom because for the great majority of inhabitants it did. However, what the majority experienced represented a very particular situation in that it involved the imposition of their socioreligious culture on the population as a whole.

The Protestant Nation

In the decades following the adoption of the Constitution, American Protestants demonstrated a remarkable ability to enhance their commonality, compatibly blending into a common ethos without diluting the independence of their various churches. Having rejected Christendom in its formal sense, Americans, with the sympathy of government at all levels, brought back many of its customs and characteristics by way of majority opinion and the collective habits and customs of their society. As historian Martin Marty has written, "Legal disestablishment meant instant reestablishment in the national ethos."[9]

If the Virginians who had lauded the pre-Constantine Church in the Roman Empire ever reflected that Christians in it had not enjoyed chaplains in the military, prayers and Bible reading in schools, or strict Sabbath legislation, they gave no indication of it. A few commentators did note that such practices were hardly congruent with religious liberty. Congressman Thomas Tucker pointed out in 1789 that proclaiming days of prayer was a religious matter and, as such, proscribed to Congress. Baptist minister John Leland hoped that the notion of a Christian commonwealth had been exploded forever. But such observations were largely ignored.[10]

James Madison had expressed apprehension that the absence of competition between religious groups would lead to a new establishment of religion, and something akin to that actually happened. In the congressional debate on the Bill of Rights, Madison noted a concern that "one sect might obtain a pre-eminence or two combine together, and establish a religion to which they would compel others to conform."[11] He had always believed that a Bill of Rights would not secure true religious liberty. Rather, the substance of that liberty would emerge from the checking and balancing of competing religious interests. However, throughout the early decades of the Republic, the major religious interests suppressed their differences in favor of a shared culture and mores.

Thus, America came to be defined as a Protestant nation, and only those who shared its common Protestantism—even while belonging to different churches—came to be seen as authentically American. This brought about a *de facto* establishment of religion perhaps more effective than many of the old legal establishments. Not until the early nineteenth century did the counterbalance Madison had foreseen as necessary for the protection of religious liberty finally emerge, in the form of Catholic immigrants.

Beginning in the 1820s, significant numbers of Catholics, primarily from Germany and Ireland, arrived in America. During the 1840s, what had been a steady stream became a torrent. By 1850, Catholicism constituted the largest religious denomination in the United States. Catholics brought with them a different culture, ethos, worldview, and religious practice. As a result, for more than a hundred years to come, the need to adjust to their presence kept the country in a turmoil that often rose to fever pitch. In turn, the hostility they encountered shaped American Catholics. In reacting to it, they transformed the nation, advanced the cause of religious liberty, and contributed to the growth of a pluralistic society.

How Catholics Challenged the De Facto Establishment

Catholics brought with them to America a different worldview, what Andrew Greeley has referred to as "the Catholic imagination." How that transformed American culture and mores largely remains to be explored. What is clear is that they challenged the dominant society in immediate and specific ways. These challenges can be grouped under three headings: church governance, education, and society and culture.[12]

Church Governance

By the time Catholics were arriving in significant numbers, Americans had generally come to believe that republican principles should apply in Church as well as in State. Most of the nation's churches were organized on a congregational basis, and that form of church governance was viewed as the only one compatible with American ways. The Catholic Church's approach to church organization was completely different. It required that churches be governed hierarchically. When groups of Catholics in various parts of America demanded that Catholicism be "Americanized" and accommodate itself to the religious customs of America by appointing congregational "Trustees" so as to bring about a more inclusive form of church government, the Catholic Church in America faced a major crisis.[13]

Catholic leaders fought this movement and preserved—even strengthened—their hierarchical form of government. Paradoxically, the triumph of a highly authoritarian religious system actually advanced the cause of religious liberty. Many Americans at the time saw the Trustee controversy as another proof of Catholicism's incompatibility with America. Moreover, participants in the controversy often saw it as a struggle to "Americanize" Catholicism.[14] However, in its historical context, the refusal of Catholics to be "Americanized" represented the first great challenge to America's self-understanding as a Protestant nation. Catholics demonstrated in practice that there was no required "American" way of being religious, and the practice of equating American identity with a religious tradition began to dissolve.

Education

Throughout much of the nineteenth century, America's public schools educated students in a common socioreligious culture. Education in these schools included reading from the King James Bible, learning common hymns, and reciting accepted prayers. Students were taught to equate England and Protestantism with liberty and progress, and Spain and Catholicism with tyranny and ignorance. Faced with Catholic objections to the inculcation of this religious worldview, school officials reacted first with genuine puzzlement, then dismay, and often with fury.

In 1859, the Boston Police Court conducted the trial of a teacher accused of severely beating Thomas Wall, an eleven-year-old Catholic pupil who refused to read from the King James Bible. Catholics demanded the right to read from the Douay Bible, and the boy had been warned by his father and the parish priest not to read the King James Version. He was systematically beaten for a period of thirty minutes before he complied. The presiding judge dismissed the case, ruling that a small group of conscientious objectors could not determine the standard for the majority. The Bible as presented was nonsectarian and thus could offend no one's free exercise of religion. To allow the use of the Douay Bible would lead to the unraveling of the bonds of society. The decision represented the sentiment of the dominant culture, which could not conceive of its accepted customs and beliefs as sectarian in any way.[15]

Catholics responded to what they saw as religious oppression in the public schools by opening their own schools—for which they soon demanded their share of public funds. Some places, particularly New York City, gave this request serious consideration, but did not grant it. Instead, the public schools gradually became more open, pluralistic, and secular.[16]

How Catholics in America set up a large system of Catholic schools is a familiar story. How this contributed to the transformation of the public schools is much less well known. The great majority of Catholic children always attended public schools. In doing so, they and their parents contributed enormously to the transformation of those schools. Over the decades, they broke down the connection between an American identity and a particular religious identity, and they put an end to the de facto establishment of religion that had been part of American education.

Society and Culture

Evangelical revivals in the early nineteenth century had helped create a common culture of American Protestantism. They had revived much of the social code that is associated with Puritanism and reinforced the observance of the Puritan Sunday. Subsequent reform movements, including the antislavery movement, shared this evangelical religion. Catholics, however, brought with them a completely different approach to life, which resulted in an immediate challenge to the dominant ethos. Philip Schaff, a well-known nineteenth-century church historian, wrote that Catholics had grown up "under the demoralizing influence of the continental Sunday, and are not yet sufficiently naturalized to appreciate the habits of the land of their adoption." [17] They differed from the dominant society's separation of work and leisure and were unaccustomed to its strict Sabbath observance. Their religion centered more on ritual and ceremony than on Bible reading and preaching. For them, card playing, consumption of alcohol, theater going, and dancing were not incompatible with their religious beliefs.

Much of the populace considered Catholics to be un-American because of their religion, but this opposition only solidified them in their devotion to it.[18] Even as many Americans proclaimed loudly—and sometimes frantically—that the nation had to be saved from the Roman threat, the country itself was changing and adjusting to the Catholic presence. Because of their numbers, Catholics could not be ignored, and they would not be assimilated. Thus, they transformed America by forcing it to adapt to them, by ending the existing identification of it as a Protestant nation. In doing so, they extended the boundaries of religious liberty.

The continued sponsorship of religious practices at all levels of government after the enactment of the First Amendment showed how much remained to be done to make the free exercise of religion a reality for all. Americans carried on those customs and practices inherited from Christendom that were acceptable to the majority of them until the arrival of so many Catholic immigrants shook the dominant culture to its foundations. However, the eventual ability of America to adjust to their presence demonstrated how fundamentally the belief in religious liberty had entered into the national consciousness and how profoundly it would continue to guide the still-emerging nation.

Nineteenth-century Catholic immigrants experienced a country well on its way to establishing a broad, nondenominational Protestantism. That they were able to achieve religious liberty for themselves and for other immigrants yet to come illustrated how deeply the principle of religious freedom was embedded in American culture and government. Their struggle to vindicate liberty for themselves also demonstrated, however, that religious liberty is not self-implementing but requires steadfast perseverance, courage, and determination.

Critics' Alternative Interpretations of the First Amendment

In 1985, Chief Justice William Rehnquist, then an associate justice of the Supreme Court, wrote a dissenting opinion in which he summed up much of the criticism of the Court's handling of the First Amendment that had emerged over the decades since 1947. Although the opinion expressed a fiercely critical attitude toward the Court's position, it also embodied the errors of the position it attacked.[19]

Two principal misassumptions have dogged discussion of the historical meaning of the First Amendment. First, critics have adopted the Court's division of the amendment into two clauses, each with a separate purpose. They agree with the Court that apart from coercion of religious belief, the entire issue of government-sponsored religion falls under the purview of No Establishment.

Starting with bad history only leads to worse. Because they are captives of the Court's faulty assumptions, critics are forced to take an opposite position. When the Court lauded the opponents of the Virginia General Assessment, its critics assumed the stance of proponents of the Assessment. When the Court proclaimed the position of the French revolutionaries with the *wall of separation* between Church and State, critics embraced the attitude of the counterrevolutionaries, arguing that the State must sponsor and promote religion.

Second, critics have assumed that if they demolish the Court's history, its First Amendment decisions must also collapse. However, as has been shown, there exists a great disparity between what the Court has actually decided and the rhetoric it has chosen for its accompanying opinions. Indeed, the Court's disastrous rhetoric is so far removed from what it has actually held that its decisions have to be examined apart from the rationale offered for them.

Evenhanded Government Support for Religion

In his 1985 dissent, Justice Rehnquist asserted that nothing in the First Amendment forbade government to promote religion "evenhandedly" or provide "non-discriminatory" aid to religion. This echoes the position of the proposed Virginia General Assessment for religion: "And it is judged that such a provision may be made by the Legislature, without counteracting the liberal principle [the free exercise of religion] heretofore adopted and intended to be preserved by abolishing all distinctions of pre-eminence amongst the different societies or communities of Christians."[20] This above argument by Virginians for evenhanded government support for religion represents a logical construct that has no basis in history or experience. As set forth in the *Federalist Papers,* American government is founded on the assumption that majorities, parties, and factions will not be evenhanded. Otherwise, there would be no need for checks and balances to make up for "defect of better motives."[21]

The lived experience of Catholics, Mormons, Jews, Jehovah's Witnesses, and other minorities flies in the face of the argument for evenhanded and nondiscriminatory government-sponsored religion. Thomas Wall was beaten, and Catholics were reviled and persecuted, because the majority regarded its own belief and customs to be nonsectarian and nondiscriminatory. To expect government to be evenhanded in its exercise of power in religious issues is to expect the impossible. The very argument that government can be nondiscriminatory in its sponsorship of religion is a violation of the First Amendment in that it advances the belief that government can know what is evenhanded in religious matters.

Religion and Irreligion

Justice Rehnquist formed his position around the argument that the First Amendment does not require government to be neutral between religion and irreligion. Once again, accepting the faulty assumptions of the position he attacked vitiated the argument. Justice Black had formulated discussion of the First Amendment in terms of neutrality rather than of powerlessness. Neutrality implies the possession of power on the part of the one who is neutral and also involves a subjective judgment. Justifying decisions on the basis of neutrality is, and has been, little more than an invitation to those on the losing side to proclaim that the Court is not neutral at all but partial to their opponents. To give judges the power to be neutral between religion and irreligion would be to endow them with arbitrary power to an extraordinary degree.

Government cannot involve itself in what it thinks is a struggle between religion and irreligion because it possesses no authority to define either. Even among adherents of the same church, differences between what is religious and nonreligious can generate the severest controversies, particularly in social, economic, and sexual matters. Oftentimes, issues that some adherents of a religion believe to be a fundamental expression of their belief will appear to other adherents of the same church as insignificant. Many religions, including Christianity, have been persecuted as being blasphemous and irreligious. What is religious and irreligious is for believers to decide. Were government to attempt to resolve that, it would be usurping a power not delegated to it.

In his concluding argument, Justice Rehnquist maintained that the No Establishment provision did not "prohibit Congress or the states from pursuing legitimate secular ends through non-discriminatory sectarian means."[22] With that, the Court's critics came full circle back to the position of the Massachusetts Congregationalists of 1780. In its constitution of that year, Massachusetts, for the secular purpose of preserving the happiness of the people and the "good order and preservation of civil government," set up a state religious system. Most Americans had already chosen a different path. They had come to believe that if virtue and goodness were to prosper, religion had to be a matter of choice, directed by the spirit and not the State. To turn it into a branch of the civil service, to use it for "secular ends," would corrupt both Church and State.

The Coalition of the Court's Opponents

On its own, an analysis of their arguments will fail either to explain or convey the passion and intensity of the Court's critics. Like the proponents of the failed Virginia General Assessment and the Massachusetts Congregationalists, whose arguments they espouse, their position more closely resembles justification of a desired system than a carefully reasoned point of view as to the relationship between Church and State. The opponents of the Court's interpretation of No Establishment come principally from two sources, one from the Protestant tradition and one from the Catholic tradition. Both engage in the same criticisms of the Court, but they differ fundamentally in their objectives.

Critics in the Protestant Tradition

The central issues that unite these critics of the Court are school-sponsored prayer and Bible reading in public education. For more than half a century, they have worked to legalize such devotions, even campaigning for a constitutional amendment to permit them. They warn that unless government sponsors religious symbols and practices that provide values for society, the country will be overrun by irreligion. In that regard, they often refer figuratively to the lack of government-sponsored religion as "the naked public square."[23]

The more extreme wing of this movement argues that government should acknowledge America as a Christian country and uphold Christianity, while urging Christians to avoid discriminating against minorities. Less radical adherents would probably argue for a Christian ethos as more accurately reflecting the American way in religion. All, however, hark back to the idea of the Protestant nation of the nineteenth century, even if somewhat modified to accommodate the concept of a "Judeo-Christian" State. Essentially, they want government to proclaim that America is a religious, preferably Christian, nation.

Critics in the Catholic Tradition

Catholics retain too much of a collective memory of their own status as outsiders to invest much ardor in the advocacy of government sponsorship of prayer or "consensus" religious exercises. Their passionate

critique of the Supreme Court arises out of a historic sense of grievance, a feeling of ill usage that derives from their having had to set up
their own schools in order to safeguard their religious liberty while
bearing the burden of supporting public schools as well. Catholic criticism of the Court centers largely on a single issue—justification of
government support for parochial schools. An understanding of this
position requires some review of Catholic development in Church-
State thinking.

Catholic Development in Understanding Religious Liberty   The social opposition, discrimination, and often outright persecution experienced by
Catholics in nineteenth-century America by no means obscured the
fact that they also greatly enjoyed the benefits of American religious
liberty. They learned to organize their churches and institutions on a
voluntary basis, neither paying for nor receiving government support,
with the result that, religiously, they prospered immensely.

American Catholics came to know firsthand that the absence of
State support for religion did not equate with a desire on the part of the
State to replace it with an antireligious or secularist ideology. They had
to contend with anti-Catholicism, and sometimes individual states or
parties within such states aligned themselves with that sentiment.
However, they did not encounter, as did their European counterparts,
a government intent on replacing religion itself with its own ideology.
They knew that as they battled to eliminate anti-Catholicism, they enjoyed an increasing freedom to grow and develop, and as they experienced increased religious liberty, so did America generally.

However, Catholics found it difficult, if not impossible, to impart the
American understanding of religious liberty to the Catholic Church in
Europe, which tended to equate the American Church-State system
with the French or European antireligious system of separation of
Church and State. The teaching of their Church in opposition to religious liberty also considerably hampered them. This doctrine was based
on the premise that error has no rights. Religious toleration, therefore,
could be accepted only as a pragmatic necessity. In countries where
Catholics formed a majority, the Church held that such toleration
should not be practiced.

One of the greatest achievements of American Catholicism has been
to reconcile religious liberty with Catholic teaching. In that effort, the

American Jesuit priest John Courtney Murray played a monumental role. Ultimately, his thought and writing would provide the basis of the American bishops' contribution to the passage of the *Declaration of Religious Freedom* enacted by the Second Vatican Council in 1965.[24]

Catholicism Proclaims the End of Christendom   In its Declaration on Religious Freedom, the Catholic Church, after sixteen hundred years, abandoned Christendom. To that point, it had advocated cooperation between sacred and secular powers to promote the common good. The State was to promote truth and to suppress error. The Declaration on Religious Freedom, however, approached the issue from a completely different point of view. It abandoned the emphasis on error and focused instead on the dignity of the individual person. This dignity demands that each person must have the right and freedom to seek religious truth. Government should be limited constitutionally and forbidden to "direct or inhibit acts that are religious." If the civil authority "presumes to control or restrict religious activity it must be said to have exceeded the limits of its power." Religion has to be "internal, voluntary, and free."[25]

With the issuance of the Declaration, the Catholic Church, influenced by the experience of American Catholics, came to accept what both Virginia's Bill for Religious Freedom and the First Amendment proclaim. All three agree that free exercise of religion means the voluntary exercise of religion, that government is limited in its powers, and that it has no authority in religious matters. The Declaration relied on the dignity of the human person; the American tradition invoked inalienable natural rights. After so many centuries, Catholics and Protestants had come into harmony on the issue of religious liberty. Christendom, in the sense of a civilization whose religious beliefs, customs, and practices were promoted, enforced, or upheld by means of secular power, was at an end. Henceforth, a religious or Christian culture would be based on the conviction, dedication, and voluntary beliefs and activities of its believers. It would no longer be a product of power; it would be a product of the spirit of God and the conviction of its adherents.

The Declaration as the Beginning of a Process   Like the Americans who enacted the First Amendment, Catholics who accepted the Declaration on Religious Freedom tended to see it as the solution to present and past problems rather than as a harbinger of change. For American Catholics, the Declaration solved their problem. They were now in harmony with American thought on religious liberty and could no longer be accused of being a threat to American values or being promoters of religious intolerance. The Declaration solved the dilemma American Catholics had experienced of adhering to religious freedom on the one hand but belonging to a Church that held a contrary teaching on the other. However, like those Americans who in 1789 declared the end of Christendom, Catholics in the 1960s tended not to anticipate the consequences of the Declaration.

Having lived with Christendom for so long, many Catholics find it difficult to abandon it altogether. Some Catholic critics of the Court, for example, attempt to save Christendom on the pretext that government is empowered to assist all religions as long as it prefers none. However, just as the First Amendment signaled a major shift in thinking that embodied many changes for State and society still to be unfolded, so the *Declaration on Religious Freedom* signals an equally profound break with the past.[26]

The argument for a system of nonpreferential government-sponsored religion leads only to a caricature of what Christendom was intended to accomplish. That system was designed to protect religious truth and suppress error, not to promote the false as well as the true, the vicious equally with the virtuous. The argument for government support of all religions equally begs the question: By what power can government determine who is religious? The *Declaration* argues for constitutional limitations on the powers of governments. If such limits prohibit government from interfering with religion, they also prohibit it from determining what is religion.

The position that government may assist all religions equally does not result from a coherent system of thought addressed to the needs of modern society. It proceeds from the assumption that government will assist those religions that are generally acceptable to the majority. On the part of Catholics, it represents a rationalization of a predetermined position, namely, that government should fund parochial schools. Their argument harks back to the Protestant Nation, modified to accommodate themselves. Ironically, some modern-day Catholics long for what their own ancestors rendered impossible. Catholic immigrants and their descendants transformed America by confronting and dismantling the

Protestant Nation. However, for several reasons, Catholic thinkers generally have not been able to grasp, let alone appreciate, that transforming achievement.

When historian Philip Schaff wrote in 1888 that Catholics "must learn to appreciate Protestant Christianity, which has built up this country and made it great, prosperous, and free," he accurately represented the prevailing attitude of the dominant culture then and for years to come. [27] Even as they fiercely resisted the pressure exerted on them by the larger society to change and conform, Catholics internalized much of the negative stereotypical assumptions that they were the products of an inferior culture, incapable of being truly American. The constant criticism they experienced and the social disapproval they encountered engendered a profound sense of insecurity, to the point where many half-believed their detractors.

Catholic scholars have largely dealt with hostility toward Catholics as the product of bigotry and prejudice. These certainly existed, but opposition to Catholicism represented much more. It characterized the turmoil of an entire society experiencing the stress of changing identity and self-definition. The major outbreaks of anti-Catholicism in America, from the Know Nothings in the 1850s to the Ku Klux Klan in the 1920s, manifested the feverish extremes of anxiety that the advent of large-scale Catholic immigration brought to the nation as a whole. The election of John F. Kennedy to the presidency in 1960 signified not only the decline of anti-Catholicism but also the fact that the country had actually redefined its identity in such a way as to render Catholicism compatible with America.

The images and assumptions that pervade American Catholic historical studies are an outgrowth of the successive waves of anti-Catholicism that swept over America until the 1960s. These images and assumptions continue to reflect insecurity and doubt—a sense of inferiority associated with the "immigrant mentality" that permeated American Catholicism in the past. They tend to visualize Catholics as having been isolated, marginalized, and devoid of any role in the development of American society. In the suppositions undergirding these studies, America tends to appear as an unchanging reality into which Catholics were eventually assimilated and to which they became accustomed.[28]

In American Catholic scholarship, religious liberty, the "separation of Church and State," is viewed as a development with which Catholics had little connection, since it had already been accomplished by the enactment of the First Amendment. In that regard, Catholics find a role for themselves only in the events that occurred in the mid-1600s, when the Calvert family made an admirable but quixotic attempt to combine Catholics and Protestants in a Maryland colonial venture.

On coming to America in the nineteenth century, Catholic immigrants found themselves confronted with circumstances that differed completely from their experiences in their home countries. They adapted to this new environment and began to create institutions unique to America, such as parochial schools and ethnic parishes. Nevertheless, Catholic studies habitually refer to this Church as an "immigrant Church," which at some indeterminate time, and by some unspecified standard, would become "Americanized." Similarly, in the minds of some Catholic scholars, the immigrants and their children had to overcome an unspecified hurdle before they could become American. Children born to immigrant parents continued to be referred to as "Irish" or "Italian," not simply as an ethnic identity but as if they were still truly not American. As American Catholics in the late nineteenth century became upwardly mobile, they absorbed the desire for respectability and the moral narrowness characteristic of the Victorian ethos that permeated the culture of the time. A popular explanation of this phenomenon among Catholics links it with Jansenism, an obscure seventeenth-century French religious movement. Here again, the explanation serves to isolate Catholics from participation in the development of American culture and society.

The image of Catholics as confined to a "ghetto" remains predominant in Catholic studies and popular Catholic imagination. It encourages modern Catholics to imagine their predecessors as having sequestered themselves from American society, as focused inward, and as having little impact on the development of the larger society.

Catholics might have lived in close communities, but that does not mean they lived in a ghetto. Two factors helped unite them and provided them with the cohesiveness and support needed to resist the enormous pressure the larger society put on them to change, to conform, and to be religiously homogenized into the nondenominational religion of the Protestant Nation. The external forces that bore down on Catholic immigrants helped them form a strong sense of identity, gave them a negative reference group against which to measure themselves, and enabled them to identify themselves by what they were not. Thus, they could present a united front to their opponents, even as they themselves experienced sharp ethnic divisions between the various Catholic immigrant groups.

Internally, the communitarian impulse characteristic of Catholicism bound Catholics together in effective and close parish communities. Whereas Protestantism had contributed greatly to the development of liberty and equality in America, Catholicism added an emphasis on fraternity. The social contract, the image of discrete individuals coming together to protect their rights, provided the founding myth for America. The image of humans as social beings, the concept that a person could not achieve a true human state apart from family and community, provided the founding myth for Catholic social mores.

These factors, one external and one internal, helped sustain Catholics in America to a point where they were not only able to resist extraordinary opposition but to drive wedges into the dominant consensus that would have excluded them. The result has led to the creation of the most participative pluralistic society the world has ever seen. Catholics did not live in ghettoes, walled off from America. Rather, they found in communal Catholicism the strength needed to face the vicissitudes of their life in America. As a result, they paved the way for the subsequent waves of immigrants that, in turn, entered and enriched the pluralism that was to become American society.

Because many Catholic scholars operate within a paradigm that separates discussion of the Catholic past from the development of America, they have set themselves on a course of documenting isolation and failure. Since the 1950s, they have devoted an enormous amount of time and energy to explaining the failure of American Catholics to create an American Catholic intellectual tradition.[29] This represents a peculiar quest in that no one has been able to define the term or provide benchmarks for its achievement. Their study of what did not happen appears to demonstrate the same deep desire for status and acceptance that characterized the "immigrant mentality."

The great changes that overtook Catholicism as a result of the Second Vatican Council included the application of historical thinking and method to Catholic thought. The Council imaged the Catholic Church as a people on a journey. It saw Catholics as discovering and understanding God through reflecting on their history and experience.

It promoted change and development in response to historical experiences and circumstances.[30]

Catholics brought to America a religious and cultural worldview that could not be accommodated by or integrated into the dominant cultural religious matrix. They helped to recreate America and to extend the understanding of religious liberty. In the historical unfolding of the free exercise of religion and in the dismantling of American Christendom, they played a crucial role. Until their modern successors discover this history, they will not be able to grasp the meaning of the abandonment of Catholic Christendom exemplified by the *Declaration on Religious Freedom*.

Summary

Discussion of the historical meaning of the First Amendment has reached a point of disarray and possible disintegration. The parties to the discussion have lost touch with the amendment's historical context, with the view of human nature that informed many who enacted the Constitution, and with a realistic assessment of how human beings act in religious matters. In dividing the First Amendment into two "clauses," each with a separate purpose, the Supreme Court made a fundamentally wrong assumption about the nature of the amendment. By equating Free Exercise of Religion with religious toleration and the absence of coercion, it cut off access to the rich historical development of religious liberty in colonial America, thereby placing an unsustainable burden on No Establishment.

Much of the modern debate about the historical meaning of the First Amendment has sacrificed history and evidence to ideology. To sustain their interpretation of establishment, defenders of the Supreme Court's 1947 pronouncement have resorted to unhistorical arguments. To prove that the framers knew of and prohibited an establishment of religion broader than a preference for one religious group, they have projected into the past the concept of nonpreferential establishments of religion. The result has been to transform the stratagems, ruses, and deceptions used by Puritans and Congregationalists to maintain their own dominance for two centuries into a new and supposedly unique American Church-State system. Modern historians have conferred on the New England Church-State arrangements a legitimacy they never possessed.

For the Court's critics, the universal understanding of establishment of religion as a state preference for one church or religion is decisive. They reason that if the prohibition of an establishment of religion forbade only a government preference, then, logically, government is free to assist all religions on a nonpreferential basis. The fact that American history provides no actual evidence in support of this logical inference does not dampen their enthusiasm for drawing it. Never has such an important historical argument rested on a logical deduction utterly unsupported by factual evidence. In the modern debate, both sides rely on logic, on abstract assessment of behavior apart from consideration of actual historical experience rather than on an appreciation of how people act and have acted, particularly with regard to religion. The concept of a nonpreferential establishment of religion or of an evenhanded government sponsorship of religion is a purely intellectual creation.

The *Federalist Papers* envisaged a government designed to make up for the "defect of better motives" on the part of citizens. The Catholic tradition adheres to the notion of original sin. Neither view warrants the "exalted opinion of human virtue" assumed by the theory of evenhanded nonpreferential government support for all religions. [31] American history demonstrates that members of dominant groups will not be welcoming or evenhanded in their dealings with groups they perceive to be different, erroneous, or challenging to themselves. In the world of experience, the concepts of nonpreferential establishments or evenhanded government sponsorship of all religions are absurd.

One of the most negative aspects of the modern Church-State debate is that its fundamental assumptions have led both sides to a conclusion that would confer power in religious matters upon the government. Proponents of the *wall* would confer on the State the same power the French Revolution did, that is, they would allow government to divide human experience into two separate spheres and make it the judge of what assists or hinders religion. This would give the State power over the Church.

Opponents of the *wall* would grant the State power to distinguish between religion and irreligion. Government could then assist what it considered religion. By definition, what it failed or refused to assist would be considered irreligion.

Either of these propositions, if followed, would lead to the same consequences as those of the French Revolution. Each would invite citizens to view the State as a prize to be captured. Supporters of the *wall,* following a purely subjective and arbitrary judgment about neutrality, about what assists or hinders religion, would use government power to eliminate all religious expression from its sphere. Opponents of the *wall* would designate critics of government-sponsored religion as irreligious. They would equate the refusal of government to determine and sponsor religious beliefs and exercises with the promotion of atheism. As formulated, the modern American Church-State debate could set up a conflict analogous to the one that the French Revolution generated between the forces of revolution and counterrevolution.

The First Amendment is not primarily a government guarantee to protect citizens in the free exercise of their religion. Rather, it is a guarantee against government interference with the religious freedom they already possess by natural right. Americans rejected both the varying Massachusetts and French propositions that to sustain a desired form of government, the State must uphold a set of religious or secularist beliefs. In doing so, they did not disparage the importance of belief and values. A people who formed a new government for the purpose of establishing justice, the general welfare, and liberty showed no lack of appreciation for the values of virtue and morality. However, Americans rejected the notion that government could achieve its own secular ends by using religious means. The most passionate support for religious liberty came from those who believed that to sustain the values and virtues of a free people, religion must be free from government manipulation. Those who would endow the State with power in religion for civic purposes are only attempting to revive the New England Church-State systems that were dying even as the First Amendment was enacted.

THE END OF CHRISTENDOM AND
THE ROLE OF THE COURTS

Although this chapter deals largely with decisions of the Supreme Court, it provides neither an overall review of Church-State cases to date nor a detailed analysis of the reasoning the Court has used to justify them. Rather, it evaluates a representative series of those decisions in the light of the historical purpose of the First Amendment in order to illustrate what might happen were the Court to decide such cases according to that purpose, which was to make explicit the ban on the exercise of power in religion contained in the original Constitution. The approach proceeds from the understanding that the amendment contains one clause with regard to religion, that the Free Exercise and No Establishment provisions of that clause do not constitute a duality but are mutual in their intent. They combine to serve the single unitary purpose of depriving government of power in religious affairs—religious belief, doctrine, devotion, or practice. If a law requires an agent of government to exercise power in the area of religion, that law is unconstitutional. Thus, the role of the Court in any instance involving Church and State is first and foremost to determine whether the contested statute or practice is secular, that is, whether it falls within the powers delegated to the State.

The purpose of this chapter is to exemplify a very different way to approach and justify Church-State decisions. Over the past half century, the justices have become entrapped in a web of confusing rules, doctrines, metaphors, and approaches that is largely of their own making. As a result, judicial reasoning has become fractured, polarized, and utterly confusing. Even constitutional experts lose their way in the maze of precedents that now surround the First Amendment. In consequence, for citizens unable to devote a significant portion of their lives to understanding this increasingly arcane specialty, the meaning of one of the most cherished liberties enumerated in the Bill of Rights becomes ever more remote. Unless the Court is able to reverse the trend of the past fifty years and connect the substance of its decisions with its justifications of them, future generations will be well advised to turn to the work of Charles Dickens for guidance as to the meaning of the First Amendment.

The approach to and interpretation of the amendment have become so much a matter of ideology that our society increasingly seeks to predict its interpretation by focusing on people rather than on the meaning of the amendment. Therefore, the future of American religious liberty is seen as depending on politics, on securing justices who adhere to one or another party in the current ideological divide. This work proposes a way not only to escape from the ideology that currently polarizes the justices but also to enable interested citizens to connect with the meaning of religious liberty and be able to evaluate contemporary Church-State contexts in the light of the purpose and meaning of the amendment.

As previously stated, the purpose is not to propose a wholesale reversal of previous judicial decisions but to escape from the chaos of the opinions that have accompanied them. This confusion has resulted primarily from bringing to the interpretation of the First Amendment a series of erroneous assumptions. It is doubly confounded by the fact that the rhetoric and reasoning employed is often utterly incompatible with the decisions reached by the same justices. Scholars and legal commentators have been of little assistance in this matter because they have continued to accept the Court's wrong assumptions and to focus only on debating its conclusions. Without a reexamination of the Court's presuppositions, the scholarship surrounding the meaning of the amendment cannot escape the swamp into which it is sinking ever deeper. Apart from the fundamental mistake of transforming the legal language of the Bill of Rights into a metaphor, much of the Court's present difficulty originates in its insistence on concentrating on the Church rather than on the State in assessing the effect of laws on religion. The following discussion will center attention on the role of government and will interpret Church-State questions in the light of the fact that government may deal only with what is secular, not with what is religious. This discussion is founded on the conviction that the First Amendment confined government to secular matters, not because those who wanted the amendment discounted the importance of religion but because they valued its importance so much that they were unwilling to allow government to manipulate it.[1]

This chapter will also deal with cases involving valid and constitutional secular laws, for example, requirements for military service, from which individuals or groups have sought exemptions because of conscience. Situations of that nature received little attention from the framers—if indeed they considered them at all. They could not have foreseen the complex web of statutes, regulations, and programs that would be woven by a government more powerful and far reaching than they could have imagined, much less anticipated. Over the ensuing two centuries, however, lawmakers and judges have increasingly been asked to grant such exemptions. Cases in this category are qualitatively different from those wherein laws are challenged on the grounds that they are unconstitutional and therefore not valid secular laws. However, because the Supreme Court has viewed itself as the guarantor of the free exercise of religion by individuals rather than as the monitor of the exercise of government power, it has conflated both categories, thereby deepening the confusion that pervades current Church–State jurisprudence.

No Government Power in Religious Matters

Traditionally, the Supreme Court has divided cases according to whether they fall under the Free Exercise or the No Establishment provision of the First Amendment. The approach used in the following pages abandons those categories and instead groups cases according to whether they involve, or could involve, government in a prohibited exercise of power in religious matters or in legislating on religious topics.

Church Property Disputes

Almost from its outset, the Supreme Court has been called upon to determine the ownership of various church properties. The earliest such cases arose out of disputed titles to property that had been acquired by grant from the English government or from one or another previously established colonial Church. In more recent times, the Court has often been asked to adjudicate property claims between conflicting groups within a particular church.

Although state courts adjudicating disputes over church property have tended to examine the religious beliefs of the contending factions in order to ascertain which represented the authentic church, the Supreme Court has consistently avoided the inclination to exercise such judgment in religious matters. For many years, the Court has recognized that it has no power to determine authentic church teaching. In 1871, it clearly acknowledged that fact when it declared that the "law knows no heresy." [2] Therefore, instead of attempting to evaluate competing claims of opposing intramural church groups, the Court has decided according to the nature of the church involved. Thus, in cases involving congregational churches, it has looked to the majority of the congregation, whereas in those entailing a centralized, hierarchical church, it has followed the decision of that church's highest tribunal. [3]

For many years and with great consistency, the Court implemented this sensible rule in line with the purpose of the First Amendment. It repeatedly refused to allow states to demand what was implicit in the Trustee controversy of the nineteenth century, namely, that churches in America had to be majority-ruled churches. Neither would it allow courts to involve themselves in the issue of implied trust and examine whether a church had remained faithful to its founding doctrine. [4]

In 1979, however, in a most important development, the Supreme Court traded clarity for confusion by decreeing that in settling church property disputes, courts could rely on "neutral principles of law." By "neutral," the Court meant "the language of deeds, the terms of the local church charters, the state statutes governing the holding of church property." These are more properly described as secular, that is, under the authority of the government to enact and interpret, rather than neutral. As for the "principles" referred to by the Court, they turn out to be no principles at all. Furthermore, the justices decreed that courts could examine fundamentally religious documents "in purely secular terms" and that the First Amendment did not require "States to adopt a rule of compulsory deference to religious authority in resolving church property disputes, even where no issue of doctrinal controversy is involved." [5]

In this case, the Court took a long step toward imposing a secularist approach on churches. It assumed that essentially religious documents can be read in purely secular terms and that the Court is the judge of religious doctrine because it has the power to decree when "doctrinal controversy" is not involved. It is possible, for example, in a controversy involving a schism in a church's highest tribunal, that the Court would have to look to existing secular documents in order to settle on a decision. However, in the case at issue, the hierarchical nature of the church was not in question. In abandoning its previous tradition, in confusing neutral with secular, and in espousing supposed "principles" that it neither defined nor clarified, the Court took a very wrong turn.

Before 1979, church property decisions handed down by the Supreme Court were exemplary. Their clarity and consistency enabled churches to reasonably anticipate the outcome of future similar ones. Such consistency could curtail much litigation and might well serve to forestall bitter religious disputes. Moreover, the Court demonstrated that the government could fulfill its secular functions and be intimately involved in the affairs of churches without exercising power in religious matters. Those church property decisions stood in utter opposition to the imagery of the *wall of separation* between Church and State and flew in the face of Justice Black's statement that government cannot "participate in the affairs of any religious organizations or groups."

No Government Restraint of Religion

If the law knows no heresy, neither can it know what is orthodox in religion. Consistently, the Justices have refused to grant public officials authority to single out, restrain in an arbitrary fashion, or prohibit the practice of religion. Many of their important rulings in this regard derived from cases brought by Jehovah's Witnesses. Particularly in the late 1930s and in the 1940s, members of the Witnesses time and time again tested and expanded the limits of religious liberty. Because they evangelized in an aggressive manner, often using methods annoying or obnoxious to others, civil authorities frequently tried to curtail or even prevent their activities. In turn, the Witnesses brought case after case before the Court to vindicate their right to act as itinerant missionaries selling and distributing their religious literature.

In its resulting decisions, the Court targeted the enactment of blanket prohibitions by municipalities, the arbitrary treatment of religious groups by public bodies, and the endowing of civic officials with power to make judgments about religion. It upheld the claims of Jehovah's

Witnesses against sweeping municipal laws banning all religious proselytizing. It forbade towns to act in a discriminatory manner, for example, refusing the Witnesses use of a public park to which other religious groups had access. It disallowed laws that permitted public officials to use discretionary power in the issuance of licenses, or that enabled them to determine what was or was not religious, or judge the character of one seeking a license.[6]

The Jehovah's Witnesses did not prevail in every case, however. For instance, the Court decided that New Hampshire could require any group to obtain permits in order to parade in a town.[7] It also upheld an ordinance of the city of Portsmouth, in the same state, forbidding the use of a particular park by them or any other religious group.[8] This last decision foreshadowed a weakness that would later emerge more clearly from the Court's jurisprudence. Although the justices consistently upheld the right to religious freedom in the Jehovah's Witnesses cases, they focused primarily on proscribing sweeping power and discretionary or discriminatory behavior. For example, they upheld the Portsmouth ordinance on the ground that the ban on park use did not discriminate between religions; yet the same ordinance conferred power on public officials to identify, single out, and prohibit religious activity. This tendency would later evolve into the Court's flawed understanding that the Free Exercise provision means that government may not coerce, discriminate against, or prohibit religious exercise in an arbitrary fashion, but that the No Establishment provision refers to government's sponsorship of religion.

In other religion cases, the Court prohibited a state from defining a film as sacrilegious and struck down a religious test for state office.[9] Over time, it has consistently forbidden government officials to make decisions on the basis of religion, to decide what was acceptable or unacceptable in religious behavior—in short, forbidden them to exercise power in religious subjects. Overall, the Court has manifested an instinctive grasp of the meaning of the First Amendment that has far surpassed its ability to arrive at a reasoned explanation of its own rulings.

Government Sponsorship of Religion

In general, the Supreme Court's decisions forbidding government restraint of religion have been met with approval or at least with little resistance. By contrast, its rulings prohibiting government sponsorship of religious belief and practice have given rise to prolonged controversy. For more than half a century, decisions striking down attempts to secure such support have been the source of much continuing commotion.

In 1948, the Court ruled that public schools were prohibited from using their buildings and administrative systems to facilitate religious instruction of students. Later, it banned school-sponsored prayer and devotional reading from Scripture in public schools. It has forbidden school districts to set up a religious orthodoxy by way of teaching biblical creationism and has disallowed the posting of the Ten Commandments in public buildings. The Court has also struck down "moment of silence" statutes designed to encourage students to pray and likewise ruled against school-sponsored prayer led by "volunteers." Further, it has banned the inclusion of religious exercises in public school gradua- ♂
tion ceremonies.[10]

Those who favor government-sponsored religion have reacted to these decisions with consternation and prolonged opposition, arguing, for example, that the Court has banished God from the nation's schools and has set up a religion of secular humanism. The source of their opposition is largely twofold. First, it arises from a persistence of the habits of mind associated with Christendom. Second, it results in part from the Court's inability to properly explain its decisions or to educate the citizenry on the nature of the First Amendment. Instead of making it clear that the amendment was intended as a guarantee that government would be powerless in religion, the rhetoric of the Court's opinions has actually encouraged contending parties to think in terms of using government power to impose their respective views of religion on society.

The Persistence of Christendom   Many Americans cling to the conviction that government, while it may not coerce belief or restrain religious practice, may nevertheless promote religion per se for the good of society. In effect, they attempt to salvage Christendom by assuming that even though the State may not decide what is false in religion, it may determine what is true or at least what is useful. Proponents of this view usually agree with the Court that the question of government-sponsored religion falls under No Establishment. However, from their historically correct argument that an establishment of religion in the past always involved a government preference for a particular religious group, they draw the incorrect conclusion that the State is free to sponsor religion on an evenhanded basis, provided it avoids favoritism.

Like their nineteenth-century predecessors, these supporters of government sponsored religion pin their hopes on "nonsectarian" beliefs and practices. They appear to assume that there exists an innermost core common to all religious faiths, adherence to which coerces none. Tending to equate religion with moral teaching, and centering their beliefs on the Ten Commandments, they cannot understand, any more than could their forebears, how government sponsorship of either could possibly violate religious freedom.

For many believers, however, the very selection of the Ten Commandments rather than, for example, the Beatitudes or the New Commandment of Christ as the fundamental underpinning of religious behavior is to embrace a specific religious perspective.[11] An approach that supporters of government-sponsored religion perceive as nonsectarian actually connects with religious controversies that go back to the beginning of Christianity.

State-sponsored religion is always preferential, always sectarian. (George Santayana wrote that one has to be religious within a particular tradition.) In the nineteenth century, the advent of immigrants brought this reality home to many Americans when Catholics, at great cost to themselves, demonstrated that what many had fervently held to be nonsectarian was indeed sectarian, even coercive. A lack of imagination prompts people to assume that what is unobjectionable to them in religion must be equally unobjectionable to others. However, the First Amendment demands that religion be freely exercised. The Free Exercise of religion means that government may not promote religion, even if some argue that such promotion is evenhanded, nonsectarian, and nonpreferential.

Results of the Inadequacy of the Court's Reasoning   By accepting the validity of the concept of nonpreferential government power in religious matters, the Supreme Court has forfeited the possibility of finding a convincing explanation for its decisions. By equating Free Exercise with no government coercion, the Court has assumed that were it not for No Establishment, government would have the power to sponsor religion on a noncoercive basis. Critics of the Court, however, advance the argument that government can do precisely that, regardless of the

No Establishment provision. They can show with certainty that at the time the First Amendment was enacted, establishment of religion and government preference in religion were synonymous. Accordingly, they conclude that the Court's apparent expansion of the No Establishment provision to include prohibition of government sponsorship on a broader basis than that of preference for a single religion is nonhistorical and erroneous.

In truth, both the Court and its critics are misled by their presupposition that the purely abstract concept of nonpreferential government power in religion was ever reflected in reality. The concept exists only in the world of logic. It has no historical substance, and in the light of human experience, it is altogether implausible.

More importantly, disregard of the historical development of Free Exercise has led the Supreme Court and its critics and defenders into a futile quarrel over the meaning of No Establishment. Both assume that Free Exercise represents a government guarantee to coerce none and tolerate all, whereas it is a restraint on—and a guarantee against—the government. In the context of the First Amendment, it is a specific declaration that government has no power whatsoever to interfere with the religious freedom citizens already possess by natural right, not even to sponsor religion in a friendly way and with no intent to coerce.

Failure to emphasize the First Amendment as an assurance of religious liberty achieved by keeping government out of religion has brought about the anomaly of all parties to the modern debate attributing power in religion to government. In envisaging a *wall of separation* between Church and State as dividing religion and government into two entirely separate spheres, the Court has encouraged those who follow its rhetoric to seek draconian government authority in religious matters. By the same token, the application of the *wall* metaphor has encouraged government officials to censor voluntary religious expression, by forbidding all religious activity within the government sphere.

The *wall of separation* metaphor can lead to the conclusion that a student's wearing a religious symbol or bringing a Bible to public school would "taint" government with religion. In a world wherein the spheres of religious activity and civil authority are completely separated, a child's drawing of religious figures for an art project in public school assumes the same gravity as the enactment by Congress of a law respecting an establishment of religion.[12] Thus, the rhetoric of the *wall of separation* invites government officials to assume enormous power to sweep the public sphere clean not only of government-sponsored religion but of every manifestation of religion.

Opponents of the ideology of the *wall,* who rightly see it as profoundly hostile to religion, accuse the Supreme Court of having imposed an antireligious system of secular humanism on the country. In fact, the Court has not actually done so. Nevertheless, such detractors are correct in arguing that its rhetoric, if adhered to in practice, would lead to the evils they deplore. The implication in the Court's opinions that it is competent to evaluate what helps or hinders religion and that the First Amendment authorized it to create two completely separate spheres of human activity is an invitation to extremism. It prompts proponents of government-sponsored religion to enlist the government in their cause, ere their ideological opponents accomplish their "relentless extirpation" of all religious belief or practice in the public realm.[13]

Thus, an amendment intended to eliminate government entirely from the exercise of power in religion has come to be interpreted by subsequent generations as justifying a struggle to recruit government to promote religious belief and devotion or to assign the practice of religion to a sphere—behind a *wall*—defined by government. The more radical members on either side of the controversy swirling around the First Amendment match each other in fervor. Each believes that the future of religious liberty depends on capturing the government for its respective religious position. In this, they are reminiscent of Catholic and Protestant combatants during the Wars of Religion that plagued Christendom.

The Court's Operating Rules

Having committed itself to a metaphorical *wall of separation* between Church and State, the Supreme Court soon realized that neither the image thereby invoked nor the rhetoric associated with it provided much practical judicial guidance. The concept of the *wall* proved inadequate as a means of clarifying the decisions of a Court that had upheld the public evangelizing activities of religious groups, ruled that they be given equal access to public parks and facilities, determined that thoroughly religious schools served a public purpose, and adjudicated quarrels between opposing church groups over the ownership of the church's property.

As early as 1952, Justice William O. Douglas, writing for the Court, declared that the First Amendment "does not say that in every and all respects there shall be a separation of Church and State."[14] Indeed, to provide themselves with more guidance, the justices developed a three-part test of constitutionality: (1) A statute must have a secular legislative purpose. (2) Its principal or primary effect must be one that neither advances nor inhibits religion. (3) It must not foster an excessive government entanglement with religion.[15]

These criteria for constitutionality flow from the Supreme Court's earlier misinterpretation of the First Amendment, brought on by its failure to appreciate the historical development of the notion of Free Exercise of Religion. The Court had incorrectly assumed that all cases involving noncoercive government-sponsored religion fell exclusively under the No Establishment provision and that the amendment dealt with government's aiding or hindering religion. Rather than providing clear guidelines for judging, the criteria tended to make the amendment mean whatever the justices said it meant. As long as the majority of the Court shared a consensus, the inadequacy of the test of constitutionality did not clearly emerge. However, with the decline of a common approach to the meaning of the amendment, the structure of opinions built on such a faulty foundation is now constantly in danger of collapsing.[16]

The difficulty with the first criterion—that a statute must have a secular purpose—is its ineffectiveness. Most government-sponsored religion is enacted for a secular purpose, usually to promote the good order of society. Article III of the Massachusetts Constitution of 1780, mandating the public support of ministers, or the defeated Virginia General Assessment Bill would easily have passed that test. However, while both were intended for a secular purpose, neither was in fact secular in that each involved religious legislation.

The most glaring defect of the second criterion—the law's principal or primary effect must neither advance nor inhibit religion—is that it is unconstitutional. The criterion endows the Court with authority in religious matters by making it the arbiter of what is good or bad for religion. It assumes judges can determine what even members of individual churches often cannot agree on. Thomas Jefferson's *Bill for Establishing Religious Freedom* would fail this test. Those in favor of the *Bill* thought its primary purpose would be to advance true religion enormously; those opposed believed it would fatally inhibit religion.

The third criterion—no excessive entanglement with religion—lacks definition. The Court has been unable to define "entanglement," let alone "excessive entanglement." If entanglement refers to government exercise of power in religion, then all "entanglement" is excessive.

Despite the weakness of its criteria, the Court's innate ability to grasp the basic intent of the First Amendment has continued to make up for its inability to set forth reasoned justifications for its decisions. In 1981, it ruled that a public university could not exclude student groups whose activity included religious worship or teaching from the use of meeting facilities available to a variety of other student groups.[17] This decision corrected the Court's earlier one allowing public officials in Portsmouth to identify, define, and exclude all religious activities from a public park. In 1990, it held that the Equal Access Act required that a public high school allow students to form a religious club on campus.[18] In 1993, it determined that public school property available for use after hours for multiple purposes be open on equal terms to religious groups requesting its use.[19]

In another case in 1993, the Court struck down a law forbidding the ritual sacrifice of animals. The town of Hialeah in Florida, in an attempt to control an unpopular religious group, had enacted a law to restrict the religious activities of members of the Santeria religion.[20] Similarly, it proscribed a Texas law under which that state had assumed discretionary power to exempt religious magazines from taxation that applied to non-religious ones.[21] It disallowed a law by which a state delegated its secular power to religious bodies by granting them control over the issuance of liquor licenses.[22] It likewise refused to allow New York, in an attempt to accommodate a group of strictly observant Jews, to draw up a special school district coterminus with the religious group's village boundaries.[23]

Although the Court has often discussed its decisions in these cases in terms of assisting, aiding, or inhibiting religion, it has with general consistency adhered to the purpose of the First Amendment by denying government officials decision-making powers in religious issues. Indeed, in several of the decisions, by upholding the voluntary exercise of religion in areas controlled by government, the Court corrected the inherently dangerous consequences of a *wall of separation* that would create "a complete and permanent separation of the spheres of religious activity and civil authority by comprehensively forbidding every form of public aid or support for religion." Where public officials sought to assume immense power to prohibit the free and voluntary exercise of religion by anyone within their sphere of control, the Court decided that the First Amendment deprived them of such authority. Fortunately, it has not followed in practice, nor allowed public officials to follow, the dictates of the theory it has espoused.

In other cases involving government sponsorship of religion, however, the Court's good insight into the meaning of the First Amendment has not served it as well as in those where government officials have attempted to assume discretionary power to define and restrict religion. In 1983, the Court upheld the power of a state to appoint and pay a chaplain to offer prayers in the state legislature. In his opinion, then Chief Justice Warren Burger relied heavily on historical precedent, on the fact that the federal Congress itself had appointed paid chaplains from its very beginning. To him, the practice represented no more than a "tolerable acknowledgment of beliefs widely held among people in the country."[24] In a dissenting opinion, however, Justice William Brennan argued that historical practice is not always determinative, and it should not have been so in this case. His dissent raised the question of the extent to which the practice of Americans in the past—as distinct from the principles they proclaimed—can be a guide to the present application of the First (or indeed any) Amendment.

Clearly, in interpreting the Constitution, the intentions of the Framers have always been significant. One must distinguish, however, between their actions and the principles they espoused. Not everything they did was in harmony with those principles, nor were they able, from the vantage point of their particular cultural and religious world, to anticipate all their effects. Future immigrants imbued with other cultural mores and professing different religious convictions would demonstrate how incompatible with religious liberty were some of the widely held beliefs and practices they encountered in America.

For the Court to set itself to judging what historical examples of government-sponsored religion are in keeping with the First Amendment is tantamount to its assuming the powers of an established Church. The purpose of those institutions was to guide the State in determining what religious practices it would sponsor. American government, however, may not sponsor any religion. The Constitution endows it with power over secular issues only.

In 1983, the Court sanctioned municipal sponsorship of a Christmas crèche as part of a general holiday display, and in 1989, it approved a city's sponsoring a menorah on public property as part of a Chanukah celebration. In these instances, the *wall of separation* imagery, in tandem with the neutrality and no–aid–to–religion tests, proved a trap for the justices. Rejecting the *wall* imagery that prohibited "all contact between government and religion" led some of them away from the central purpose of the First Amendment, namely, assurance of no government power in religion, and to a preoccupation with government aid to religion.

Government contacts with religion are multifarious; however, they need not lead to exercise of government power in religion. To maintain the no–aid–to–religion rule and still reach the outcome it wanted, the Court majority had to obviate the religious significance of the displays it upheld. It found in 1983 that the effect of the Christmas crèche in promoting religion was only "indirect, remote, and incidental" and in 1989 that the Chanukah menorah would be of only "intangible" benefit to religion and represented the secular aspect of the celebration.[25] In these and other cases, the Court endowed itself with expertise in religion.

In 1988, however, in another context, the Court rightly pointed out that judging what was "central" and, by implication, what was "peripheral" to religion did not fall within its purview and that to attempt to decide these issues would "require us to rule that some religious adherents misunderstand their own religious beliefs."[26] Nevertheless, the Court's earlier and later decisions regarding the crèche and menorah displays and, indeed, its "purpose and primary effect" rule, pointed it in that very direction. For the justices to assume that people will go to the considerable trouble and expense of bringing a case to the Supreme Court for the sake of something merely trivial and of only indirect and intangible assistance to religion amounts to second-guessing on their part. It implies that the Court knows better than the litigants what is central and important to religion.

Subsequently, in 1995, the justices dealt with a public religious exhibit that had not been sponsored by local government—the unattended display of a cross in a public square by the Ku Klux Klan. Justice Antonin Scalia, writing for the Court, was able to avoid some of the confusion previously associated with decisions regarding public displays of religious symbols: If the government allowed the unattended display of other symbols, including religious symbols, then it could not discriminate on the basis of the particular source of an item to be displayed. It could forbid all, but it could not forbid some because of the disagreeable nature of their religious sponsors.[27]

Government Assistance to Religious Schools

The issue of government assistance to religious, mostly parochial, schools has come before the Supreme Court and lower courts with greater persistence than any other Church-State matter in modern times. Here again, the Court has proven unable to bring its decisions and its rationale for them into harmony. In these cases, this disparity emerged in 1947 when Justice Black declared that although the First Amendment had created a *wall of separation* between Church and State, New Jersey could nevertheless reimburse parents for the cost of transporting their children to parochial schools. Four dissenting justices at the time excoriated Justice Black's decision. They took issue not with his reasoning as to the meaning of the No Establishment provision but with his application of it. They declared that the Court, having asserted that government could not aid one or all churches, had proceeded to violate its own pronouncement. In their focus on the matter of government aiding religion, both majority and dissenters combined to steer Church-State jurisprudence onto a path that could only lead in the wrong direction.

Actions of government, beginning with implementing the First Amendment itself, assist religion in a multitude of ways. Accepting parochial school education as fulfilling a public purpose enables religious groups to instruct children in religion in a way that would otherwise be impossible. Churches benefit from tax exemptions enjoyed by all non-profit groups. As discussed earlier, religious groups are assisted by the right to evangelize in public places, to avail themselves of public parks, streets, and facilities. To permit government to deny to churches "every form of public aid or support for religion" would be to endow the government with immense authority, not deprive it of power as the First Amendment was intended to do. The following discussion of public assistance to religious schools will focus on that topic from the point of view of the exercise of government power in religion, something the amendment prohibits, not the consequences for churches of valid secular laws, something the amendment forbids the courts to assess.

Over the past fifty years, the Court has considered a veritable multitude of laws enacted to assist religious schools, and the increasing popularity of school voucher programs indicates the issue will continue to come before it. In this admittedly thorny matter of government assistance to religious schools, the Court has followed a winding path. The justices found in favor of bus transportation to such schools but against field trips from them. They have allowed states to provide them with textbooks and, most recently, computers but not with maps or film projectors. Further, the Court has permitted therapeutic and remedial assistance to students at religious schools but struck down salary supplements for their teachers. It has forbidden tuition grants but allowed tax deductions for school expenses. In some cases, the Court has ruled that a state can pay for standardized testing of parochial school students, and in other similar cases, it has ruled the opposite.[28]

To proponents of wide-ranging government assistance to religious schools, the Court's wobbly path has been infuriating and at times ludicrous. There is indeed much to find fault with in its decisions. However, advocates of such aid manifest their own form of inconsistency. While excoriating the Court, they, too, have adopted reasoning quite at odds with their actual practice. Their inconsistencies are evidenced by what they have supported.

In 1968 and 1969, the states of Pennsylvania and Rhode Island provided salary subsidies for teachers in parochial schools on the grounds that the secular and religious components of those schools were clearly separable. The schools themselves eagerly accepted that government assistance. Nevertheless, in 1972, the Catholic bishops of the United States issued a statement on Catholic education asserting that religion should be integral to the entire program of a Catholic school, should permeate the whole school curriculum, and should not be merely a separate subject apart from the others. Yet the bishops continued to defend vigorously the Pennsylvania and Rhode Island state subsidy statutes, in spite of the fact that both states had forbidden the use of funds for, in the words of the Pennsylvania statute, "any subject matter expressing religious teaching."[29]

The salary subsidy issue exposed the fact that the promoters of government support for parochial schools equaled the Court in drastic incongruity between theory and practice. In reality, the schools were very willing to make a clear distinction between their secular and religious activities. In theory, however, they adhered to a completely different standard. For example, when the National Labor Relations Board asserted jurisdiction over religious schools, the Catholic bishops argued that because religion was so integral to parochial school education, such jurisdiction would inevitably involve a government agency in making religious decisions. In 1979, the Court agreed with them.[30] The import of the arguments advanced by supporters of government assistance to parochial schools is that those schools can be thoroughly religious, completely subject to religious control, and—apart from specifically religious activities—completely tax supported. In practice, however, this reasoning has no more guided the Court's critics than has the image of the *wall of separation* guided its decisions. The knotty problem of government assistance to religious schools will come close to solution only if and when the Court and its faultfinders are each able to harmonize their respective reasoning and action.

In 1968, the Supreme Court upheld a state law under which New York provided textbooks to religious schools. In that case, Justice Byron White, writing for the Court, stated his belief that the secular and religious components of those schools were quite separable and that the state could support the secular educational function.[31] Soon after, Pennsylvania and Rhode Island won approval of salary provisions for teachers in their parochial and religious schools. Nevertheless, the Court was unwilling to accept the guarantees involved, and in 1971, it struck down both those states' salary subsidy provisions. In his opinion for the majority, Chief Justice Burger wrote that his decision was not predicated on a belief that the schools would use public money for religious purposes but rather that they would be unable to separate their religious and secular functions. He affirmed that the schools constituted "an integral part of the religious mission of the Church."

In this assessment, the Court was completely correct, certainly as regards the history of religious schools. However, the judgment was one that the First Amendment renders the Court, as such, powerless to make. Parochial schools have certainly been "an integral part of the religious mission of the Church," yet the education provided by them is accepted by the State as fulfilling a public function. The proper question for the Court, therefore, is this: If a state assists parochial schools in fulfilling the public purpose of educating children, will that assistance involve government in making religious decisions?

Chief Justice Burger's opinion announced the judgment of the Court, but a harsher concurring opinion, written by Justice Douglas and seconded by Justice Black, brought to the surface fundamental issues underlying the religious school decisions. In it, Justice Douglas quoted, with approval, an anti-Catholic author on the subject of parochial school education:

> The whole education of the child is filled with propaganda. That, of course, is the very purpose of such schools, the very reason for going to all the work and expense of maintaining a dual school system. Their purpose is not so much to educate, but to indoctrinate and train, not to teach Scripture truths and Americanism, but to make loyal Roman Catholics.

Justice Douglas himself wrote, "One can imagine what a religious zealot, as contrasted to a civil libertarian, can do with the Reformation or with the Inquisition," and commented that to free the public schools from denominational control was "admirable as seen through the eyes of those who think like Madison and Jefferson." [32]

Justice Douglas's observations revealed two disparate influences operative in many of the Court's Church-State decisions. The first of these embodied the tag end of the great strife and disharmony rampant in America from the beginning of major Catholic immigration. At that time, for the majority of the nation's population, "Americanism" had come to mean the blend of culture and religion they were familiar with and that had contributed so much to their liberty, both civil and religious. Because Catholics did not share in that religion and culture, it was believed they could never be true Americans. But Catholics had long since demolished that equating of religion and culture with American identity. They had already established the fact that to be American involves no religious requirement.

The second influence Justice Douglas's comments brought to light was an ideological mindset that had emerged from the French Revolution, rather than the American Revolution, and had entered Church-State jurisprudence by way of the *wall of separation* metaphor. This tended to link "Americanism" with an ideology characteristic of those who assumed that there was an "approved" American way of thinking.

In such a scenario, the justices subtly become not those who confine government to its proper secular sphere but defenders of the "Revolution." They are led toward a preoccupation with what is religious instead of what is secular, to the tacit assumption that religious schools are somehow less "American" than other schools. Such schools become analogous to Dissenters in eighteenth-century England.[33] Dissenters could not be suppressed, but although the established Church of England had to tolerate them in a grudging manner, it ensured that they would be disadvantaged in every way possible and seen as un-English and a blot on the desired uniformity of the nation. By analogy, justices sometimes see parochial schools as Justice Douglas did—as something to be tolerated but deprived of every possible government encouragement. However, the proper focus of the Court is secular, not religious. Moreover, the Constitution does not require the imposition of a uniform ideology on the country. To the extent that a religious school fulfills a secular purpose, the role of the government should be to assist it in achieving that purpose—without involving itself in religious decision making—so that the education it provides its students will enable them to contribute most effectively to the good of society.

Justice Douglas served on the Court for thirty-six years, beginning in 1939. During that long period of service he saw himself—and came to be seen by others—as a staunch defender of liberty. However, he also illustrated in startling fashion the mischief that a misunderstanding of the history surrounding the First Amendment, combined with an ideological approach derived more from the French Revolution than the American and set in a context of anti-Catholic prejudice inherited from the past, can produce.

The misunderstanding of history began with the interpretation of the Virginia General Assessment controversy, on which much of the modern Court's interpretation of the First Amendment is based. Virginians rejected this plan because it would have given government power in religion, namely, to pay ministers to preach. Modern judges, however, have made use of this historical refusal of Virginia to allow its government to enact religious legislation in order to justify their own examining of the religious impact and consequences of secular legislation. To follow the logic of this approach to its conclusion would endow the government with unlimited power instead of curtailing its authority as the amendment was intended to do. For example, states have consistently proposed legislation to assist parochial or religious schools in fulfilling their public and secular purpose of educating children. Judges have often looked at the religious implications of such secular laws, such as the provision of secular educational materials to parochial schools, and have decided that their religious effect would be to save the churches involved a great deal of money. Were this reasoning applied consistently, local fire departments could not respond to fires in church buildings. Although putting out conflagrations is a secular activity, their doing so in such instances would save churches the very large sums involved in rebuilding burned structures, which would indeed assist and advance religion.

Such would be the consequence of a *wall of separation,* and such are the consequences of interpreting the First Amendment as a ban on government aid to religion instead of as a prohibition of the exercise of government power in religion. Fortunately, the Court has not followed the logic of its misunderstanding. However, as Justice Douglas's opinion illustrated, the negative views of Catholics inherited from the American past give this faulty history and reasoning a very negative cast when applied to Catholic schools.

Propagating the concept that public schools represent the official and truly American way of educating children while parochial schools represent merely a concession to dissenters introduces a false division between both systems. The vast majority of Catholic children have always attended and continue to attend public schools. Public and parochial schools equally fulfill a public purpose, and neither is less "American" than the other. Governments can assist both in fulfilling that purpose but must recognize that in doing so they may not enact religious legislation or make religious decisions.

Over the course of a generation, the Court and the proponents of assistance to religious schools have come closer to agreement. In part, this development has resulted from an increased willingness on the part of the Court to concur that parochial schools can indeed separate their religious from their secular components. However, it has also been achieved by the participation of both bodies in an elaborate fiction that government may not assist religious schools but may assist parents in their choice of schools for their children. In this way, public tax money supposedly does not aid religious schools themselves.

The need for such a stratagem arises out of the Court's original misinterpretation of the First Amendment as intended to prevent government assistance to religion, whereas the original purpose of the amendment was to prevent the exercise of government power in religion. In turn, that misconstruction has led supporters of aid to religious schools to engage in endless mental contortions in order to accommodate the Court's reasoning.

Wrong assumptions have tended to drive arguments further from reality. The essential issue to be considered is whether money given to religious schools to fulfill their public purpose will involve government in making religious decisions. Governments may not simply give money to parents for the education of their children and fail to monitor the schools involved. States may not allow tax money to go to schools that are racially discriminatory, that are incompetent, or in which the curriculum followed does not fulfill a public purpose. In 1983, the Court ruled that a school that engaged in racial discrimination was not eligible for tax exemption.[34] The need for the kind of mental gymnastics that attempt to turn public tax money into private income can be eliminated by a realization that the First Amendment limits judges to determining what is secular, not what is religious or advances religion or religious schools.

In an important decision in 1997, the Court demonstrated just such a realization. Reversing a previous ruling, the justices held that public school teachers could provide onsite remedial instruction at parochial schools.[35] In effect, they found that those teachers were engaged in secular education and that their presence in the parochial schools involved no participation in religious matters by a state authority. Their decision demonstrated that the justices had come to trust that the schools in question could indeed separate their religious and secular components. The ruling has been much lauded by advocates of government support for religious schools as a model for the future, which indeed it is, manifesting as it does that government may support all those elements of religious school education that are clearly secular and thereby fall within the scope of its regulation and oversight.

The preponderance of the evidence since the Court disallowed the Pennsylvania and Rhode Island teacher subsidy statutes indicates that parochial schools are willing in practice to accept this understanding in return for public funding. In Wisconsin, the state supreme court has already upheld a voucher program for the city of Milwaukee, which provides an "opt-out" clause that allows participating students to be exempt from involvement in any religious activity.[36] This amounts to a de facto recognition of the distinction between secular and religious curriculum components. In a school whose curriculum was permeated by religious teaching, choosing the "opt-out" provision would amount to a student's leaving the school entirely.

Advocates of government assistance to religious schools, however, while criticizing the Court, have failed to face the disparities in their own position. They, too, need to bring their argument and practice into better agreement by acknowledging the ratio that must exist between the amount of government assistance provided and the extent of religious control exercised. Justice Douglas noted that the problem of religious control "loomed large where the Church controls the hiring and firing of teachers." The same would apply to the selection and retention of students. A school supported at public expense must also be commensurably subject to public controls, and the Court has decided that a state may not delegate its proper power to churches. A publicly supported religious school cannot reasonably demand that it be free from oversight by public agencies or at liberty to determine its hiring or firing of staff according to the degree to which they carry out the religious mission of the school. Accession to either demand would render the state—as a financial supporter of the school—a participant in religious decisions, something forbidden to government in America.

To a great extent, therefore, the solution to the conundrum of government assistance to religious schools depends on whether those schools choose to define themselves as religiously pervasive in their curriculum or as religious sponsored. If they define themselves as completely religious, they can demand a great measure of independence and autonomy, but the amount of government support for which they will be eligible will be strictly limited. On the other hand, if they define themselves as religious sponsored, if they are willing to make a clear distinction between their secular and religious components, they can receive extensive government assistance. Such schools can also validate many of the arguments advanced in favor of government aid to parochial schools by providing choice, quality education, particularly for poor families, as well as competition in education.

The topic of school choice occupies a prominent place in recent public discussion. However, in the matter of government assistance for religious schools, the most fundamental choice must first be made by the schools themselves in the light of a realistic assessment of the consequences of such aid.

For its part, the Court can bring renewed and clearer guidance to the controversial issue of aid to religious schools by grasping the unitary intent of the First Amendment, thereby perceiving that the specific objective of its framers was to prevent government from involving itself in religious decisions. Whether secular legislation advances religion is not for government to decide. Such an understanding on the part of the Court will free advocates of government aid to religious schools from the need to engage in mental twists and turns in order to conform to the Court's tortured reasoning. For over a century and a half, state governments have been willing to accept that thoroughly religious schools fulfill a public purpose. The effect of that decision has been to aid those schools enormously. The Court's role is to monitor and explain the consequences to the State, not the Church, of any government programs designed to assist religious schools. The justices need to assess the "principal or primary effect" laws have on the State, not on the Church.

Claims for Exemptions for the Sake of Conscience

The following discussion focuses on the exercise of government power—the proper subject of the First Amendment—in the context of the extent to which the State should grant exemptions from a valid secular law when citizens claim its application would inhibit them in the free exercise of their religion. It proceeds from the understanding that cases of this nature are qualitatively different from those dealing with laws that violate the First Amendment by involving government in the exercise of power in religious matters. The justices of the Supreme Court, however, often discuss such cases as if they had been appointed the guardians of the religious liberty of plaintiffs, particularly those belonging to small, unconventional religious societies.

The Flag Salute Cases

As they did with regard to the issue of the free exercise of their religion, Jehovah's Witnesses provided an occasion for a fundamental examination of the issue of exemption of religious believers from laws they find themselves unable in conscience to obey. Members of that religious body refused to salute the United States flag, citing their belief that such

an action was forbidden them by the biblical prohibition against wor-
shiping graven images. During the 1930s, this refusal led to the expulsion of many of their children from America's public schools, in which
each school day began with that practice. The plight of two of them,
Lillian and William Gobitis, aged twelve and ten respectively, came before the Supreme Court in 1939 in what was the first Flag Salute case.[37]

Writing for the Court, Justice Felix Frankfurter set forth the principal argument against claims of conscience exempting anyone from obey-
ing the secular law. He asserted unequivocally that a valid law, one not
aimed at the religious beliefs of individuals but rather designed to promote the common good, must be obeyed. Otherwise, the laws of the
land would become discretionary, subject to evaluation by the nation's
multiplicity of religious groups as to which to obey and which to ignore on the basis of conscience. Such power of choosing would deprive
legislatures of the ability to govern and thus lead the country into
chaos. As long as people had the right to believe and practice their chosen religion, their liberties were not infringed. The Flag Salute law in
question had the crucial secular objective of promoting national unity,
the very basis of national security. Therefore, it had to be upheld.[38]

The Court's decision led to the expulsion of even more children, to
more publicity, and to public indignation. As a result, within three years,
Witnesses were able to bring the issue before the Court again. This time,
Justice Robert Jackson, writing for the majority, took a different approach. Without questioning either the importance of national unity or
the power of the government to promote respect for the flag, he asked
whether government could require children to express the belief demanded by the salute. In effect, he sought to determine whether the
law was a valid secular one. He decided it was not. He reasoned that by
imposing a belief, the law invaded the realm of "intellect and spirit,"
whereas the purpose of the First Amendment was to render the imposition of belief off-limits to government power.[39]

Thus, in the second Flag Salute case, the Court ruled that government may not impose any belief—secular or religious—on its citizens.
In its earlier decision, it had held that while freedom to believe was absolute, freedom to act was of necessity limited. However, a majority of
the justices had by then come to see the action involved in saluting the
flag as symbolic, that is, its sole purpose was the expression of belief.
The realm of government is secular and measurable; the realm of belief

is beyond its power to compel. Therefore, government could not force persons to perform—or to refrain from performing—symbolic expressions of belief.

In a passionate dissent to Justice Jackson's opinion, Justice Frankfurter defended both his position in the earlier Flag Salute case and his commitment to religious liberty. He reiterated his argument that individual religious judgment may not serve as a criterion for whether or not to obey a law. He asserted that the children involved were free to believe whatever they liked, that the law in question merely forced a child "to make what is to him an empty gesture and recite words wrung from him contrary to his religious beliefs."[40] This illustrates in startling fashion why judges should not attempt to evaluate what advances or impedes religion. The book of Maccabees describes people dying agonizing deaths because they refused to perform a symbolic gesture. The early Christian martyrs died similarly for refusing to perform a simple symbolic act of burning incense before an idol, a gesture that the authorities thought was of little significance. In both instances, initial sympathy on the part of officials often turned from frustration to fury because they could not fathom why people were willing to die for "an empty gesture." The history of civilization is replete with examples of the inability of governmental officials to understand the nature and power of religious belief.

In his majority opinion in the second Flag Salute case, Justice Jackson questioned whether patriotism could be promoted by compulsion: "To believe that patriotism will not flourish if patriotic ceremonies are voluntary and spontaneous, instead of a compulsory routine, is to make an unflattering estimate of the appeal of our institutions to free minds." This sentiment illuminated a similarity between the issue of the flag salute and the principal religious issue that had divided America at the time of the enactment of the First Amendment. The majority of the people in Massachusetts had believed then that unless the state government required a "compulsory routine" of religious activity, citizens would abandon religion and with it civility, morality, and values. Only constant reminders of a "future state of rewards and punishments," they thought, would provide a basis for public morality. The majority of their fellow Americans, on the other hand, had rejected routine government sponsorship of religion, believing that it could only lead to a deadening external conformity. Instead, they embraced the more radical Reformation idea that only religion free from the manipulation of government and guided by the spirit of God could provide the basis for true liberty and virtue.

In the long run, the Flag Salute cases did not serve as a guide for deciding claims for exemptions from valid secular laws because the Court determined that compulsory Flag Salute statutes were not valid secular laws. Nevertheless, they did raise—and call attention to—questions that would be dealt with in subsequent cases involving claims for exemption from other laws, all of which would be considered valid secular legislation.

The majority opinion in the second Flag Salute case had noted that children's refusal to salute the flag presented no clear and public danger to national unity. In a concurring opinion, Justice Frank Murphy observed that the benefits to society of forcing children to salute the flag did not appear to him to outweigh the negative effects of suppressing their liberties. By balancing competing interests, the Court, over successive years, worked out a principle to be applied in deciding claims for exemption. In its responses to requests to be exempted from working on a religious Sabbath, as well as other claims for religious exemptions, the Court generally relied on the rule that unless government could prove a "compelling state interest" for applying the law, a claimant should be exempted for the sake of conscience.[41]

This practice lasted until 1990, when the Court radically reversed direction. In a decision that involved the illegal use of peyote for religious purposes, Justice Scalia, writing for the Court, declared that generally applicable laws not aimed at religious belief and practice must be obeyed. To allow exceptions would—as Justice Frankfurter had argued years before—make individual conscience the judge of the laws of the land and invite anarchy. The remedy for those objecting to particular laws was to be found in the democratic political process. With this decision, the Court returned to the reasoning of the first Flag Salute decision.[42]

Like its ruling in the first Flag Salute case, the Court's decision in the peyote case gave rise to an enormous outpouring of critical public opinion. In response, Congress enacted the Religious Freedom Restoration Act of 1993, restoring the "compelling interest" test. In 1997, however, the Supreme Court considered a claim by the Catholic Church in San Antonio that the Religious Freedom Restoration Act justified its expanding a church building located in the city of Bourne, even though that city had designated it a historical monument and refused to grant a building permit. The Court struck down the Religious Freedom Restoration Act in its application to the states, on the ground that in passing it, Congress had exceeded its authority.

The View from History

Does the history surrounding the enactment of the First Amendment indicate that the Framers intended that exemptions from generally applicable laws would be granted for the sake of conscience? Of necessity, the justices have argued inconclusively about this proposition because the Framers did not anticipate it. Their experience had never required them to address the question. They were aware of refusals to pay religious taxes, but those who objected to such levies did not petition for exemptions but rather argued for the abolition of laws they regarded as unjust and oppressive. The First Congress did briefly consider exemption from military service for conscientious objectors, but it rightly saw the matter as one to be dealt with by the states, since at the time it would only have come up with regard to service in state militias. Many years before, Quakers had caused quite a stir by refusing to remove their hats as a sign of deference, to swear oaths, or to serve in the military. However, those controversies were as far removed in time from the experience of the Framers as the late nineteenth-century Mormon controversies about polygamy are from the present.[43]

State laws having to do with religious liberty included provisions against acts of licentiousness or behavior contrary to good order and public peace. Just what specific acts their authors had in mind were never stated. They may have been reacting to accusations that the free exercise of religion would destroy the sanctity of oaths and public morality, or they may have been copying a formula from each other. In any case, the lack of evidence about their specific intentions points to the conclusion that they had either failed to consider those terms carefully or were unaware of any particular instance of what they warned against.

In the absence of direct historical evidence, the issue of exemptions for the sake of conscience must be debated within the context of what is most compatible with the spirit and purpose of the First Amendment. Originally, the amendment was enacted to deprive the government of power in religious matters. To exempt people from the application of a law they claim would prohibit their free exercise of religion when the government has no compelling interest in enforcing the law is more in harmony with the original purpose of the amendment than is the current interpretation—the "secular rule" that if laws are valid secular laws, they admit of no exemption apart from what the legislatures choose to provide. Although that rule may appear to represent a logical, straightforward, and readily applicable solution to the problem, in reality it raises several difficulties.

First, the rule assumes that a law is not aimed at the restriction of religious belief or practice. Once more, this assumption places the assessment of a religious matter in the hands of secular judges. Assessing whether legislators intended a law to inhibit religion differs from assessing whether the law in fact does so. Judges might well be able in certain cases to assess the motives of lawmakers. However, apart altogether from its authors' motives, whether a law is aimed at religious practice or belief is for believers to decide. Similarly, judges have no ability to determine what is religiously "neutral" because the evaluation of religion is beyond their ken. Religious practices for whose sake believers seek exemptions are often those that judges are least capable of understanding or appreciating. History exemplifies how poorly they are able to discern if a law is aimed at religions that are unconventional or unpopular. Nevertheless, the fact that religious believers are the proper determiners of the effect of laws on their beliefs and practices by no means compels the government or the courts to accept their conclusions. Moreover, judges are not prohibited from examining the possibility of fraud or collusion on the part of the claimant.[44] Judges or lawmakers properly determine what is a compelling state interest. What they are forbidden to determine is the effect of a secular law on a religious practice.

Second, the "secular rule" assigns the vindication of religious liberty to the political process, even though the purpose of the Bill of Rights is to withdraw certain rights from that political process, to proclaim them as inalienable, anterior to government, and not dependent on the will of the majority. Moreover, the Court argues that the free exercise of religion for some minorities must be sacrificed to majority opinion without a review by the justices of the relative importance of the law in question. This is to equate religious liberty with the greatest happiness of the greatest number.

Third, the "secular rule" is ineffective as a rule of law in that it proposes relief for majorities who have no need of it and avoids relief for minorities who do. If they could find relief in the democratic process, minorities would have no need to appeal to the courts.

In enacting the First Amendment, the Framers certainly did not intend to exclude all secular legislation that might impede or prohibit the free exercise of any religion. However, they could not have imagined subsequent requests for exemptions from valid secular laws, nor could they have anticipated the power and regulatory reach of modern government. Legislatures may now, by way of generally applicable secular laws, wipe out the free exercise of religion for small and politically unimportant groups with far greater efficiency than intolerant regimes of the past could have done by way of religious persecution.

One of the objections to granting exemptions from secular laws for the sake of conscience is that the courts would be overwhelmed by a multiplicity of religious believers claiming exemptions from the variety and complexity of modern legislation. The history of the Supreme Court indicates that the justices can avoid this consequence.

For more than a century, the Court has dealt with a varied but steady stream of claims for exemption from laws for the sake of conscience.[45] In the late nineteenth century, the justices refused an exemption from the criminal law for those who wished to practice polygamy for religious reasons. In the early twentieth century, they refused to grant exemptions from citizenship requirements for those who would not participate in the military. Such conscientious objectors could not get an exemption in order to attend a public university, to gain a law degree, or to gain admission to the bar. Moreover, the Court later held that conscientious objection did not justify a refusal to pay taxes intended for the support of the military.

The Court also refused to permit Jehovah's Witnesses to allow their children to engage in the sale of religious literature in the streets at late hours in violation of child labor laws. It held that states could enforce Sunday closing laws even if they disadvantaged Jews, who observed a different Sabbath, and that children could be given blood transfusions over the religious objections of their parents. The justices denied an exemption from military rules to an officer who wished to wear a yarmulke while on duty, and they also declined to grant a petition by Native Americans that the government be prohibited from building a road through land the latter held to be sacred.

Nevertheless, the Court has also shown considerable solicitude for conscientious objectors. It has upheld citizenship for one who would not serve in the military but who would serve as a noncombatant. During the Vietnam War, it went to great lengths to grant exemption to conscientious objectors who based their objections on personal convictions that diverged greatly from traditional religious beliefs and faith in God. However, when a Catholic asked to be exempted from military service in that particular conflict because he saw it as an unjust war, the Court had no difficulty in denying his claim. Though they did not say so, the justices probably perceived a clear and compelling interest in not exempting a member of one of the largest religious groups in the country.

Generally, the Court has been unsympathetic to requests for exemptions from Sabbath work, although it has been particularly solicitous to ensure that those who could not work on Sundays or were dismissed for their refusal to do so received compensation. It permitted Amish parents to take their children out of school after the eighth grade but refused to exempt members of the same group from paying Social Security taxes. It would not exempt a religious objector from being assigned a Social Security number. However, the Court did grant relief to one who petitioned for religious reasons not to have her picture on her driver's license and to another who objected to displaying his state's motto, "Live Free or Die," on his license plates.

From these numerous cases, the only discernible pattern to emerge is that for more than a hundred years, judges have tended to balance the interest of individuals and the State in favor of the latter. The history of requests for exemptions from valid secular laws gives no indication that consideration of them will lead to anarchy.

James Madison rightly saw that competition between—and balancing of—different sects and interests would preserve religious freedom. The "secular rule" removes the Supreme Court as a party to this balancing process. It values logical consistency over experience and the true interest of the State. The wholesale persecution of children following the decision in the first Flag Salute case is a salutary warning that the Court's withdrawal from even reviewing claims for exemptions for the sake of conscience can lead to a drastic imbalance against the rights of individuals. In the absence of court review, legislatures have little incentive to avoid insensitivity, callousness, or ignorance in making valid laws that can severely affect the free exercise of religion on the part of those who have little influence in the democratic process. It would be tragic if the Court, having itself decided that Congress may not preempt it in interpreting the law, continued to refuse to review valid secular laws that prohibit such free exercise.

Summary

The Supreme Court's 1995 decision upholding the right of the Ku Klux Klan to exhibit an unattended display of a cross in a public square dramatically typified the end of Christendom.[46] For sixteen hundred years, the cross had been central to that system. Upholding the right of a group to use this symbol to proclaim the antithesis of Christianity signified again the end of the system that had begun with Constantine.

The decision also sent a radical message to traditional Christian believers that they could not rely on the power of government to uphold beliefs traditionally shielded by Christendom. If public facilities are open to some, they must be open to all. The fate and prosperity of different religious beliefs is dependent on the faith and conviction of their proponents. Even two hundred years after the enactment of the First Amendment, this message continues to pose a great challenge for many religious adherents.

Some believers have approved court decisions that reverted to government-sponsored religion of the past. Those decisions carried equally drastic implications for religion. For example, the Court upheld the public sponsorship of a Christmas crèche as long as the religious figures in it took their place alongside clown figures, teddy bears, and a talking wishing well. It allowed public sponsorship of a menorah but only by redefining it as a cultural instead of a religious symbol. Such rulings reach to the very heart of the meaning of free exercise and its historical development over four centuries. They illustrate in concrete fashion the radical Reformation argument that when the State sponsors religion, it assumes the power of the Church and tailors religion to its own purposes.

One of the most serious deficiencies of the Court's Church-State decisions is that while the justices have generally upheld the practice of religious liberty, they have been unable to educate the country on the meaning of that liberty. Overall, the Court's opinions, together with academic writings and popular commentaries, have led the country away from an appreciation of religious freedom as it developed before—and was embodied in—the First Amendment. They have tended, over the past half-century, to immerse people in protracted wrangling rather than to lead them in the new direction signaled by the Constitution and the First Amendment. Indeed, in 1947, the Supreme Court catapulted different groups into a struggle that continues to the present, as one contends with another for the support of the government and the Court, in order to enforce its own views of religion on the nation.

The Court's critics have rightly opposed its faulty reasoning and its extravagant rhetoric; unfortunately, they would also overturn its decisions. Their alternative would be to enable majorities to use government power to implement their religious beliefs and devotions. However, forcing people to attend a religious service as a condition of participating in a public school graduation, or subjecting them to prayers or devotional reading of Scripture as a condition of attending public school classes or functions, will advance neither virtue nor religious liberty. For the government to turn a public building, park, or square into a religious shrine so that all citizens have to acknowledge one group's religious devotion is only to return America to the religious impositions of the past. The State belongs to all, and exists to serve all. The government and its agents may not engage in either the promotion or the denial of religious belief. A teacher in a public school or university may not pronounce on the truth or falsity of Catholicism any more than a city may inscribe a rosary on its municipal seal to proclaim itself Catholic.

Those who argue that government may sponsor religion provide two justifications for their position. First, they proceed from a standpoint of utility and claim, as did some Americans at the time of the enactment of the Constitution, that since religion fulfills an important public purpose, government must sponsor it for the good of society. Absent coercion, government may employ religious practice for the public good. Justice Scalia espoused this argument in his criticism of the Court for disallowing government-sponsored prayer at a graduation: "To deprive our society of that important unifying mechanism in order to spare the nonbeliever what seems to me the minimal inconvenience of standing, or even sitting in respectful nonparticipation, is as senseless in policy as it is unsupported in law."[47]

Justice Scalia's argument hearkens back to the Act of Toleration, assuming as it does that the government has power in religious matters but is forbidden to use that power to coerce. It balances the religious desires of majorities against their inconvenience to minorities. If, according to the definitions of judges, the majority is not coercive, the minority should not be able to thwart its will. Moreover, in addition to making an assessment about religion, this argument prescribes how the minority should react in the face of majority oppression. It misses entirely the development of the tradition of religious liberty as freedom from government use or manipulation of religion as an instrument of government policy. It also ignores the fact that for more than a century, Catholics fought the imposition of religious practices that the majority thought were compatible with religious liberty.

The second justification for government-sponsored religion rests on a questionable reading of history and tradition. In 1983, Chief Justice Burger found the appointment of a religious chaplain in a state legislature represented merely "a tolerable acknowledgment of beliefs widely held among the people of this country." The practice has had an unbroken two-hundred-year history. Justice Anthony Kennedy has argued that government support of religion is an accepted part of the cultural and political heritage of America from its beginning.[48]

That government has for more than two hundred years, and at all levels, supported and advanced religion is unquestionably true. However, to argue that longevity has made such practices acceptable is to sanitize history. Government-sponsored religious practices going back to the Founders and approved by a high percentage of the population at the time amounted to an informal establishment of religion, one that caused untold hardship for Catholics, Jews, and others who did not share the cultural and religious ethos of the majority.

Justice Sandra Day O'Connor has argued repeatedly that No Establishment prohibits government from making adherence to a religion "relevant in any way to a person's standing in the political community."[49] Religious practices of ancient lineage sent a message to Catholics in the past that they were not and could not be true members of that community. Their refusal to participate in ancient and revered religious practices that were utterly foreign to them boggled the minds and imaginations of those who found such observances wholly unobjectionable. They, too, saw a refusal to participate in such religious exercises as the obstinacy of a troublesome minority trying to disrupt the accepted customs of the majority. To contend that longevity validates government-sponsored religion is to ignore a long history of oppression of outsiders.

Perhaps the greatest dilemma the Court faces is that while the critics of some of its decisions seek to replace religious freedom with the tyranny of the majority, many of the defenders of those decisions would use the Court's rhetoric to implement a different tyranny. The latter would turn an amendment designed to take power away from government into permission for government officials to define religion and determine its proper sphere. They would turn a prohibition of government-sponsored religion into a ban on even voluntary religious expression within range of their power. They would endow themselves with competence to determine what advances religion and would not only oppose government-sponsored prayer but also eliminate all prayer from the sphere of government power. Those who would define the free exercise of religion as belonging to church and home, or behind a figurative *wall* of their making, would delegate to themselves authority to regulate religious behavior comparable to that exercised by established churches in the past.

Advocates of government-sponsored religion are often driven by the belief that it constitutes the sole alternative to the establishment of an ideology hostile to religion. They are motivated by the conviction that their opponents have captured public education and instilled in it their own antireligious sentiments and secularist ideology. They are correct in their assessment that much of the Court's rhetoric seems to justify the creation of such a system. They are incorrect, however, in offering a solution that depends on the creation of state-sponsored religion. Moreover, they are misled in their insistence that the Court has already validated the imposition of secularist, antireligious beliefs.

The logical division of the First Amendment into two clauses with separate purposes has bifurcated the Court's vision and brought on a conflict that should not exist. Instead of seeing itself as bound to help religion on the one hand and not help it on the other, the Court needs to recover the unitary purpose of the amendment, which is to prohibit the exercise of government power in religion, not to prohibit aid to religion.

For more than fifty years, supporters of government assistance to parochial schools have been learning the art of constitutional contortion to accommodate themselves to the vagaries of the Court's reasoning in order to render those schools eligible for public aid. In this regard, the Court needs to explain not what helps or hinders religion but rather the limits of what the State can do without involving itself in religious decisions. Its proper role is to determine the effects of government assistance to parochial schools on the State, not on the Church. Clarifying the fact that public assistance to religious schools may not and need not bring government to the point where it has to exercise authority in religious matters will prove a help in resolving this contentious issue. It will enable religious schools to anticipate the consequences of public assistance and provide them with a clear choice, namely, whether to remain as largely self-supported, religiously integrated schools, or to become religious-sponsored schools. There already exists a lengthy tradition of religious entities carrying out secular tasks for government. As far back as a century ago, the Court decided that government could contract with a hospital belonging to a Roman Catholic religious society to perform secular tasks specified and regulated by government.[50]

For their part, advocates of government assistance to religious schools need to abandon the habits of mind inherited from Christendom. The notion that parochial schools can be fully religious, totally church controlled, but paid for by government pertains to the world of established churches. In that world, the State, having selected an official church, entrusted to it many tasks, including that of education. Such churches, however, were the creation of the State and controlled by it. In a world in which the State is forbidden to exercise power in religious matters, government may not support teachers and students financially and yet be excluded from decision making about the status of either. If a government is substantially involved in financing a school, the area of its involvement must be amenable to government oversight.

Courts need to recognize that their role is to declare what is secular. They need to clearly convey this limitation on government to advocates of public support for religiously sponsored schools. This mutual understanding will allow both judges and advocates of public support for parochial schools to abandon the charades they have engaged in. It will also liberate judges from the need to become "experts" in religion,

pretending that government assistance is not really—or is only of incidental—assistance to religious schools. It will permit promoters of this
support to abandon the pretence that public aid assists only parents, not
schools. No constitutional alchemy can transform public taxes into
funds to be disbursed solely at the discretion of individuals. Thus, government may not give public funds to parents without monitoring how
and where they are used.

Seemingly endless attempts to devise a proper separation between
the secular and the sacred remain the fundamental source of modern
Church-State confusion. The image of a neutral Supreme Court places
it between two contending parties, the Church and the State. Yet the
Constitution demands that it concern itself only with the State. Despite
many pronouncements to the contrary, the Court proceeds on the assumption that the First Amendment created a new right to religious
liberty and that the justices are the guardians of that liberty. Justice
Scalia wrote in 1990 that the "free exercise of religion means, first
and foremost, the right to believe and profess whatever doctrine one desires." This is not quite accurate. First and foremost, the amendment is
a guarantee that government will not interfere with the freedom citizens already possess by natural right. Primarily, it is focused on what
the government does not do, rather than on what individual citizens
do. As Hamilton so shrewdly foresaw, bearing in mind that the First
Amendment is a negative against government is a source of never-end-
ing difficulty.

There is no conflict in the First Amendment because it was designed
for the single purpose of keeping the government from interfering in
religious matters or from sponsoring religious beliefs and practices. A
statute that involves government in the exercise of authority in religion
is unconstitutional. Many laws, however, beginning with the First
Amendment itself, have a major impact on religion. Evaluating that impact, that is, determining whether a secular law advances or impedes
religion, is forbidden to courts by the same amendment.

If adherents of a religious tradition claim that the effect of a valid
secular law is to impede or destroy their religious liberty, the Court
should be open to reviewing exemptions from that law. The First
Amendment emerged out of a desire to protect religion from government power. Therefore, allowing exemptions from secular laws when,
as determined by the Court, the government does not have a com-

pelling interest in enforcing them is in harmony with the purpose and spirit of that amendment. Even if the laws in question are valid secular ones, the Court should not rule out the possibility of their review if they prohibit the free exercise of religion.

The ancient fear that without government sponsorship religion will decline and society will lose all sense of values still fuels the argument for State involvement in religious matters. A government founded to "establish Justice, insure domestic Tranquility, provide for the common defense, promote the general Welfare, and secure the blessings of Liberty" does not lack fundamental values. Centuries ago, Roger Williams pointed out that forbidding government to exercise authority in religion, what he called the First Table, did not preclude it from upholding values for society. The Constitution is rooted in the radical assumption that government must confine itself to its own proper sphere. By interfering in religious matters, it would usurp authority and corrupt religion. Values are not advanced by sacrificing the religious liberty of the minority to the desire of the majority to establish its own religious customs and devotions by means of government power. Religion has been—and will continue to be—the source of values and virtue. But America is committed to the principle that only if religion is freely and voluntarily chosen and exercised will it nurture the conviction and virtue necessary to a free people.

CONCLUSION

At the beginning of the modern controversy about the meaning of the First Amendment, Justice Wiley Rutledge wrote: "No provision of the Constitution is more closely tied to or given content by its generating history than the religious clause of the First Amendment."[1] For decades now, scholars and commentators adhering to radically differing interpretations have claimed that history unquestionably supports them. Yet no other provision of the Constitution has generated so much more rhetoric than reasoning. No other article of the Bill of Rights exists in a greater fog, resulting from the triumph of passion and party over historical imagination and evidence. No other amendment in its modern application varies more from the view of human nature that generated it.

Many writers confidently argue that the First Amendment's prohibition against an establishment of religion leads to the principle of separation. On close examination, however, this principle of separation means only that there shall be no establishment of religion. The Supreme Court committed itself to the rhetoric of a high and absolute *wall of separation,* but it has had to admit that this metaphor represents no more than whatever the justices say it represents.

The attitude of historical certainty can often only be maintained in combination with a vagueness that allows for grand historical pronouncements unchecked by any consideration of inconvenient evidence. For example, the Court decided that the meaning of No Establishment was tied to the Virginia General Assessment controversy of the 1780s. However, that notion of history overlooks the fact that the Virginia controversy was not about the meaning of establishment of religion at all.

Historians circumvent this inconvenience by contending that James Madison, who wrote the *Memorial and Remonstrance* against a General Assessment in Virginia, also wrote the First Amendment and that he embodied his opposition to government-sponsored religion therein. They maintain that Americans in 1789 were divided as to whether an establishment of religion meant preferential government assistance to one religion or nonpreferential government aid to all religions. Madison's modern champions vehemently proclaim that he wanted to prohibit both possibilities. This position, about the historical meaning of an establishment of religion, can only be sustained by a determined exercise of selective memory.

Justice Brennan once observed, "If the Framers of the amendment meant to prohibit Congress merely from the establishment of a 'church,' one may properly wonder why they didn't so state." However, Madison, the Framer, did precisely so state. He proposed banning a "national religion." He wanted to forestall a situation whereby "one sect might obtain a pre-eminence, or two combine together and establish a religion to which they would compel others to conform."[2] Much contemporary writing on the history of the First Amendment holds that the majority of the senators wanted exactly what he set forth, namely, a ban on a national establishment, but that in fact Madison then led the fight against it. Such assertions lead to the conclusion that Madison was initially confused and underwent a change of heart in the course of the debates in the First Congress. Yet no evidence exists to indicate that he (or anyone in the Congress) experienced such a profound "conversion" about the meaning of an establishment of religion.

The immediate cause for this apparent wholesale subversion of history lies in a loss of the meaning of the free exercise of religion and a refusal to accept the overwhelming evidence of what Madison and his contemporaries meant by an establishment of religion. They defined it as a government preference for one church or religion. By reading a logical inference into this historical description of establishment, modern scholars have utterly misinterpreted that evidence. The common historical prohibition against the establishment of any one religion in preference to another never signified—much less embodied—an im-

plied consent to government power in religious matters short of preference. The more basic source of the modern confusion about the history of the First Amendment, however, is to be found in the assumptions about human nature, behavior, and historical experience that
underlie the debate.

The claim that government can or did support many religions on a
nonpreferential basis relies on a view of human nature radically different from that shared by Madison and his contemporaries. The premise
that a popular government could exercise the kind of objectivity,
virtue, and dispassionate fairness necessary to evenhandedly assist multiple religions assumes that "the better angels of our nature" are more
in control of human affairs than a study of history would warrant.

By contrast, Madison discerned in religion one of the principal
sources of faction and oppression. He did not rely on a belief in government fairness and benevolence as any guarantee of liberty in religion. Rather, he perceived that tyranny resulting from "the defect of
better motives" would be prevented by a "multiplicity of sects" checking and balancing each other.

The wisdom of experience had convinced Madison and his contemporaries that government involvement in religious matters inevitably
led to preference. That had been the meaning of establishment of religion throughout history, and that is still the case. Arguments in favor of
evenhanded, nonpreferential government support for religion were
then and are now intended to justify majority religious preference.

The selectivity and vagueness that have guided modern understanding of the socioreligious atmosphere of America at the time the First
Amendment was enacted characterize the ongoing discussion of the
amendment's broader historical context. Justice Brennan—quoting Justice Felix Frankfurter—probably exemplified a widely held understanding of history prior to the American Revolution that the "Framers
of the First Amendment were sensitive to the then recent history of
those persecutions and impositions of civil disability with which sectarian majorities in virtually all of the colonies had visited deviation in the
matter of conscience."[3] If "recent history" therein refers to the experience of the framers, then that interpretation is entirely wrong.

A century earlier, in 1689, England had passed the Act of Toleration,
which introduced into America a degree of religious liberty unknown
before that time. Thus, the Framers' awareness of religious persecution

and torture was vicarious in nature. Qualitatively, the Church-State issues familiar to them were comparable to those of our own time. They dealt with attempts by majorities or interest groups to capture the power of government on behalf of their own religious views and customs. They experienced the arrogance of majorities as well as petty harassment of and condescension toward—rather than severe persecution of—minorities. They were familiar with the use of government-sponsored religion for the supposed benefit of society. In Virginia, Baptists had been jailed for preaching without a license. (Jehovah's Witnesses would suffer the same fate in twentieth-century America.) But the Framers had no first-hand knowledge of severe religious persecution, and Protestants—virtually the entire population—suffered few civil disabilities on account of religion.

Over the course of the two centuries that have elapsed since the adoption of the First Amendment, America has been the scene of harassment, persecution, and suffering for the sake of religion far exceeding any such behavior that occurred in the century preceding its passage. Mormons had to leave the United States for Utah (which at the time belonged to Mexico). Catholics had to form parallel institutions to protect their religious liberty, their children suffered beatings in the public schools, and their institutions were threatened or burned. Jewish children were punished and ostracized for refusing to participate in Christian celebrations. In the twentieth century, Jehovah's Witnesses suffered persecution perhaps not matched in severity since earliest colonial times.

Organizations such as the Know Nothings, the American Protective Association, and the Ku Klux Klan, rather than government entities, are known to have been responsible for much religious persecution. But there is little doubt that their cause was often assisted by at least local government connivance, as well as by the public support of a cultural-religious system that classified immigrants and minorities as outsiders and encouraged harassment and oppression of them.

To laud government's continuing sponsorship of religious practices and argue that the passage of time has justified it is to lose sight of the enormous struggles that have been waged to preserve the ideal of religious liberty embodied in the Constitution. To contend that the sieve of history has strained out the more noxious of those practices, so that the remainder constitute an acceptable residue, is to lose sight of the fact that the founding generation also eliminated practices it considered pernicious and retained those acceptable to the majority, thus setting the stage for future travail.

The genius of the American system of religious liberty, however, lies not just in eradicating persecution but in enabling dissenters to vindicate their rights. Moreover, it has engendered a deep-seated belief in an "American spirit" that continues to challenge American society to implement the ideal embodied in the First Amendment—that government must not exercise power in religious matters.

In their assumption that the purport of the Free Exercise of Religion is clear and straightforward while that of an Establishment of Religion is subtle and elusive, modern historians and jurists have reversed history. The meaning of establishment of religion had never varied prior to the enactment of the First Amendment, and Americans at the time universally agreed on its definition. The concepts of religious liberty and free exercise of religion, however, had undergone a fundamental transformation.

William Penn has as good a claim as anyone to the title of Founder of American Religious Freedom, yet he is almost as unknown in modern Church-State discussion as Roger Williams was in colonial and revolutionary America. Although Madison and Jefferson provided some of the most enduring public statements about religious liberty, Penn provided the votes for it. Without the astonishing example of Pennsylvania and those other states influenced by it, the proponents of voluntary religion in America would never have been able to overcome the long established belief of Christendom that, in the absence of government support for religion, civilization would collapse.

Pennsylvania kept alive the radical evangelical conviction that only a religion free from government interference could be truly godly. In the early eighteenth century when Americans were led back to that conviction by the Great Awakening, they found encouragement in Pennsylvania's example. Because modern historical discourse about the First Amendment has sought enlightenment almost exclusively in the more secular writings of Madison and Jefferson, it has missed the intense religious conviction that motivated the development of religious liberty in America.

Failure to comprehend Americans' steadily widening and deepening understanding of the meaning of free exercise of religion has led historians and judges back to the pragmatic tradition of toleration, as exemplified by Massachusetts. Justice Scalia mistakenly argued that Madison did not hold that the proposed Virginia General Assessment violated the "free exercise" provision of Virginia's Declaration of Rights, but both Madison and the most popular petition by far of the assessment controversy certainly did.[4]

Virtually all participants in the modern Church-State controversy imply that, consistent with the Free Exercise provision of the First Amendment, government may exercise power in religious matters if it does not coerce or prefer. They differ solely as to whether the No Establishment provision prohibits such an exercise of power. Only when they rediscover that Free Exercise means freedom from government sponsorship of religion or exercise of power in religious matters will they be able to connect accurately with the amendment's founding history.

In the absence of an appreciation of this radical, Reformation-inspired, religious conviction, the pull of Christendom reasserts itself. People are prompted to call upon government to assist religion. They contend that in failing to sponsor it, government demonstrates hostility toward it. Again, this argument proceeds from the notion represented in the Massachusetts Constitution of 1780 that since religion is useful to society, the State should sponsor it. In that context, religion is perceived as a moral system embodying a collection of tenets. However, for those who understand or experience religion as a matter of conviction, as a profound and personal relationship with God, use of the heavy hand of government to impose a utilitarian, moralistic view of religion is a fundamental violation of their right to the free exercise of it. Government's use of religion as a social tool, the imposition of a notion of religion "approved by" politicians or public officials, and the direction of contrived prayers to a composite god all vulgarize religion and deaden the spirit of true religious faith.

As the Supreme Court has rightly declared, a secular State is not ipso facto an antireligious State. By refraining from interference in religious matters, government respects the God-given freedom of individuals to follow their own chosen religious beliefs and practices. On the other hand, a government that would erect a *wall of separation* between Church and State is not a secular State. A government that would evaluate laws on the basis of whether they advance or impede religion would thereby assume to itself both competency and supremacy in religious matters.

Governments that really did build a *wall of separation* between Church and State, that enforced a "complete and permanent separation of the spheres of religious activity and civil authority," have brought untold misery to humankind. Such regimes have imposed their own orthodoxies and ideologies. They have determined where, when, and how religion would be exercised, and have used their power to confine it and prevent it from competing with "official truth." Relying on the rhetoric of totalitarianism adds nothing to our understanding of American religious liberty. Persistent adherence to the metaphor of a *wall of separation* between Church and State serves only to strengthen the position of those who maintain that until government returns to State sponsorship of religion, it will continue to promote atheism.

Americans have escaped the hardship and distress of religious absolutism in large part because they live within a governmental structure erected by Framers who understood and respected history and who looked to human experience in carrying out the immense task that fell to them. The time is long overdue for modern historians and judges to consider the background of the First Amendment in the same way. As early as 1654, inhabitants of Rhode Island wrote delightedly to their friends and relatives in England that they had almost forgotten what tithes and religious taxes were. Did their descendants abandon the Rhode Island tradition of religious liberty when they petitioned in 1790 against the establishment of any "particular religious sect or society"?[5] According to the dominant major modern interpretation of an establishment of religion, those Rhode Island petitioners would have approved government's sponsoring religion, so long as it avoided preference. In fact, they would have condoned no such thing. They were using the definition of establishment common to America at the time, which never implied that prohibiting a preference for one religion would allow nonpreferential support for all religions. The conclusion that it did imply that derives only from the analytical world of logic, not the empirical world of observation and experience.

Understanding that the First Amendment prohibits government from exercising power in religious matters—either by promoting government-sponsored religious exercises or, conversely, by walling off religion from the public sphere—will liberate America from the numbing controversies that have troubled it for decades. For religious believers, a clear comprehension of government's lack of competence and authority in religious matters will lead to the rediscovery that religion is above all a matter of the spirit, not of the secular authority. Only those who possess a deep religious conviction founded in that spirit can bring to public life the religious values that have helped sustain—and will continue to nurture—the public realm. For those who serve in government, the realization that the First Amendment is designed to deprive them of power in religious matters will help them to understand that it does not confer upon them the authority to deny the free exercise of religion to individuals or groups, to determine what advances religion, to pronounce on the truth or falsity of religion, or, above all, to impose ideologies of their own using government authority. For American Catholics in particular, knowledge of the crucial role played by their predecessors in the development of American religious freedom will provide a clear perception that the appreciation of the dignity of each individual, so central to the *Declaration on Religious Freedom,* is fundamentally intrinsic to freedom from government-imposed or government-sponsored religion.

Those who approve of government-sponsored religious practices sometimes argue that people are "free to ignore them."[6] On the contrary, no one should be required to ignore an action by government that it is not empowered to take. That response too closely resembles the attitude of the early Puritans. To those who objected that some who had come for liberty refused it to others, the Puritan authorities replied that dissenters had full liberty to go elsewhere! Fortunately, they generally did not go elsewhere, but instead stayed to challenge, to check and counterbalance the tyranny of the majority, and in doing so to extend the reach and understanding of religious liberty. To attempt to perpetuate Christendom is to ignore their struggles, to deprive individuals of freedom and dignity, and to turn back in the direction of religious tyranny. It represents a sorry loss of historical wisdom and imagination.

NOTES

1. Setting the Context

1. Austin Flannery, O.P., ed., *Vatican Council II: The Conciliar and Post Conciliar Documents* (Collegeville, Minn.: Liturgical Press, 1975), 799–812.

2. *Everson v. Board of Education,* 330 U.S. 1 (1947). Cases are also available and searchable online at *http://www.findlaw.com/*. On the present crisis, see, for example, Steven D. Smith, *Foreordained Failure: The Quest for a Constitutional Principle of Religious Freedom* (New York: Oxford University Press, 1995), v–vi.

3. The Court's use of history in its 1947 interpretation has been critiqued from the beginning and continues to be the source of discussion. See especially Mark DeWolfe Howe, *The Garden and the Wilderness: Religion and Government in American Constitutional History* (Chicago: University of Chicago Press, 1965) and Douglas Laycock, "Nonpreferential Aid to Religion: A False Claim about Original Intent," *William & Mary Law Review* 27 (1986): 875–923, for a review of many of these works. Critics of the Court have generally failed in their arguments because they have attacked the Court's conclusions while accepting its erroneous assumptions.

4. See Thomas S. Kuhn, *The Structure of Scientific Revolutions* (Chicago: University of Chicago Press, 1970), for an explanation of paradigms. This work does not provide a review of the available literature on the First Amendment, much less a critique of that literature. My intention is neither to ignore nor dismiss previous literature but to build on differing assumptions than those accepted by almost all modern writers on this subject. Neither does this work proceed on the assumption that arguments originating under a different paradigm are all false. For a recent bibliography on Church and State, see John Witte, Jr., *Religion and the American Constitutional Experiment: Essential Rights and Liberties* (Boulder, Colo.: Westview Press, 2000), 341–361.

5. Although Constantine radically altered the relationship between Christianity and the Roman Empire, he did not establish the Christian religion. However, those Americans who in the later eighteenth century rejected Christendom traced establishment back to Constantine. For more on Christendom, see Peter Brown, *The Rise of Western Christendom* (Oxford: Blackwell Publishers, 1996). For discussion of the meaning of the end of Christendom for religion, see Douglas John Hall, *The End of Christendom and the Future of Christianity* (Valley Forge, Pa.: Trinity Press International, 1997) and Stanley Hauerwas, *After Christendom? How the Church Is to Behave if Freedom, Justice, and a Christian Nation Are Bad Ideas* (Nashville: Abingdon Press, 1999).

6. Edward Gibbon, *The History of the Decline and Fall of the Roman Empire,* 7 vols., ed. J. B. Bury (1909; reprint, New York: AMS Press, 1974), 1:31.

7. Norman F. Cantor, *The Civilization of the Middle Ages* (New York: HarperPerennial, 1994), 270, 400. See also Eamon Duffy, *Saints and Sinners: A History of the Popes* (New Haven: Yale University Press, 1997).

8. This work will maintain a distinction between secular and secularism or secularist. Actions that are secular are seen as those within the limited purview and competence of the government. Secularism is an ideology by which the secular power assumes authority to exclude religious expression altogether or confine it to the area defined for it by the secular state. For a brief review of theories about religion and politics, see David Hollenbach, S.J., "Religion and Political Life," *Theological Studies* 52 (1991): 87–106.

9. Jefferson also wrote that the federal government was "interdicted by the Constitution from intermeddling with religious institutions, their doctrines, discipline, or exercise." Letter from Thomas Jefferson to Rev. Samuel Miller (January 23, 1808) in Anson Phelps Stokes, *Church and State in the United States,* 3 vols. (New York: Harper & Brothers, 1950), 1:490–491.

10. William T. Hutchinson et al., eds., *Papers of James Madison,* 17 vols. (Chicago: University of Chicago Press, 1962–), 11:129–130. See also Leonard W. Levy, "No Establishment of Religion: The Original Understanding," in Leonard W. Levy, *Judgments: Essays on American Constitutional History* (Chicago: Quadrangle Books, 1972), 219 n. 330. This essay provides a concise summary of the historical events surrounding the enactment of the First Amendment. A revised version of this essay can be found in James E. Wood, Jr., *Religion and the State: Essays in Honor of Leo Pfeffer* (Waco, Tex.: Baylor University Press, 1985), 43–83. See also Michael McConnell, "The Origins and Historical Understanding of Free Exercise of Religion," *Harvard Law Review* 103 (1990): 1473–1480. Robert A. Rutland, "Framing and Ratifying the First Ten Amendments," in *The Framing and Ratification of the Constitution,* ed. Leonard W. Levy and Dennis J. Mahoney (New York: Macmillan, 1987), provides a short overview of this subject.

11. *Federalist Papers* 84. The *Federalist Papers* are available on the Internet at many sites. The version used here is provided by the Gutenberg Project.

12. On the discussion of the need for amendments, see Thomas J. Curry,

The First Freedoms: Church and State in America to the Passage of the First Amendment (New York: Oxford University Press, 1986), 194–196, 198.

13. Akhil Reed Amar, *The Bill of Rights: Creation and Reconstruction* (New Haven: Yale University Press, 1998), 39, points out that whereas the First Amendment took away power, it is read as if it stated that "Congress shall have power. . . ." Two articles, Rudra Tamm, "Religion Sans Ultimate: A Re-Examination of Church-State Law," *Journal of Church and State* 41 (1999): 252–284, and John A. Fliter, "Keeping the Faith: Justice David Souter and the First Amendment Religion Clauses," *Journal of Church and State* 40 (1998): 387–409, provide examples of opposite arguments in the modern Church-State debate. In that debate, each side rightly fears that the triumph of its opponent's argument would undermine the First Amendment. The first would allow the government to pursue "legitimate secular ends through nondiscriminatory sectarian means." *Wallace v. Jaffree,* 472 U.S. 38, 113 (1985). It would allow government to promote the religion acceptable to the majority and define religious liberty as the ability of minorities to ignore this. *County of Allegheny v. ACLU, Greater Pittsburgh Chapter,* 492 U.S. 573, 664 (1989). The second would allow the State to impose an ideological "faith" on the Church, based on a metaphorical wall of separation. This faith, if implemented, would endow public officials with power to identify, define, single out, and prohibit voluntary expression of religion on the part of individual citizens and groups. See discussion of the cases *Widmar v. Vincent,* 454 U.S. 263 (1981); *Lamb's Chapel v. Center Moriches Union Free School District,* 508 U.S. 384 (1993); *Board of Education of the Westside Community Schools v. Mergens,* 496 U.S. 244 (1991) in chapter 4. Fortunately, the Supreme Court has implemented generally neither position, and neither represents the purpose of the First Amendment.

14. Leonard W. Levy et al. eds., *Encyclopedia of the American Constitution,* 4 vols. (New York: Macmillan, 1986), 3:1439–1440.

15. See *Lee v. Weisman,* 505 U.S. 577, 629, 646 (1992). Jesse H. Choper, *Securing Religious Liberty: Principles for Judicial Interpretation of the Religion Clauses* (Chicago: University of Chicago Press, 1995), views the Court as a protector of religious liberty. See also Jesse H. Choper, "Separation of Church and State," and Leo Pfeffer, "Religious Liberty," in Levy et al., *The Encyclopedia of the Constitution,* 3:1650–1658, 3:1538–1545.

16. *Employment Division v. Smith,* 494 U.S. 872, 877 (1990).

17. *Federalist Papers* 84.

18. Matters of style were of considerable concern at the time, such as whether the Bill of Rights should be listed separately or integrated with the text of the Constitution. See Joseph Gales, ed., *The Debates and Proceedings of the Congress of the United States [Annals of Congress]* (1834), 1:735.

19. *Lemon v. Kurtzman,* 403 U.S. 602, 612 (1971).

20. Oliver Wendell Holmes, *The Common Law* (Boston: Little, Brown & Co., 1881), 1. See also Vincent Crapanzano, *Serving the Word: Literalism in America from the Pulpit to the Bench* (New York: New Press, 2000), xxiv, 197–356.

21. Curry, *First Freedoms,* 134–148, 163–177, reviews that involvement.

22. "It is necessary in a free exercise case for one to show the coercive effect of the enactment as it operates against him in the practice of his religion. The distinction between the two clauses is apparent—a violation of the Free Exercise Clause is predicated on coercion while the Establishment Clause violation need not be so attended." *School District of Abington Township v. Schempp,* 374 U.S. 203, 221 (1963). McConnell, "Origins and Historical Understanding," provides a justifiably notable account of Free Exercise. In its beginning assumptions, this work differs from that article.

23. Laycock, "Nonpreferential Aid to Religion," 906, writes: "That many of the Framers' generation understood the difference between exclusive and nonpreferential establishments seems as certain as can be for a proposition about what people were thinking two hundred years ago." The certainty of this assertion can only be maintained by projecting a modern concept of non-preferential establishment into the past, sustaining it by a reliance on textual analysis alone, and discounting and ignoring the overwhelming body of historical evidence to the contrary. The empirical evidence demonstrates that the opposite was true. See chapter 2, notes 14–16 following.

24. The proposed formulas can be found in Laycock, "Nonpreferential Aid to Religion," 880–881 and in Witte, *Religion and the American Constitutional Experiment,* 242–243.

25. For the first group, see Laycock, "Nonpreferential Aid to Religion"; and Leonard W. Levy, *The Establishment Clause: Religion and the First Amendment* (New York: Macmillan, 1994). For the second, see Robert L. Cord, *Separation of Church and State: Historical Fact and Current Fiction* (New York: Lambeth Press, 1982); Chester James Antieau, Arthur T. Downey, and Edward C. Roberts, *Freedom from Federal Establishment: Formation and Early History of the First Amendment Religion Clauses* (Milwaukee: Bruce, 1964); Arlin M. Adams and Charles J. Emerich, "A Heritage of Religious Liberty," *University of Pennsylvania Law Review* 137 (1989): 1559–1671; and *Wallace v. Jaffree,* 472 U.S. 38, 91–114 (1985).

26. For a summary of comments from contemporaries on the unimportance of the Bill of Rights, see Gerard V. Bradley, *Church-State Relationships in America* (New York: Greenwood Press, 1987), 88.

27. All the states that formed constitutions during the revolutionary period, all the states that requested an amendment regarding religion, and all other Church-State discourse at the time equated an establishment of religion with a government preference.

28. *Federalist Papers* 10, 51.

29. Historical writing on Church and State tends to be dominated by the need for logical coherence at the expense of historical evidence. One of the principal methods of finding this coherence is by way of what lawyers often refer to as "Law Office history," the selection of evidence to fit a theory. An example of this is the wholesale avoidance of the fact that all Americans in

1789 thought of an establishment of religion in terms of a government preference. Less commented upon, however, has been the tendency to posit hypotheses and then proceed to act as if they were sustained by historical evidence.
For example, Americans argued that "no particular sect or society ought to be
favored or established by law in preference to others," therefore, government
could promote all religious sects and societies on a nonpreferential basis; or the
First Amendment deprived the federal government of power in religious matters because Americans wanted the states to have power over religion; or James
Madison radically changed his views on Church and State during his lifetime
or even between 1786 and 1789. Historical arguments are very often judged on
the basis of fiat or decree, whether the author finds them "persuasive" or
"compelling" or "plausible." In this, modern scholarship follows a famous
precedent:

> The first thing he did was to furbish some rusty armour which had be-
> longed to his great-grandfather and had lain mouldering in a corner. He
> cleaned it and repaired it as best he could, but he found one great defect:
> instead of a complete helmet there was just one simple morion. This
> want he ingeniously remedied by making a kind of visor out of paste-
> board, and when it was fitted to the morion it looked like an entire hel-
> met. It is true that, in order to test its strength and see if it was sword-
> proof, he drew his sword and gave it two strokes, the first of which
> instantly destroyed the result of a week's labor. It troubled him to see
> with what ease he had broken the helmet in pieces, so to protect it from
> an accident he remade it and fenced the inside with a few bars of iron in
> such a manner that he felt assured of its strength, and without making a
> second trial he held it to be a most excellent visor. (Miguel de Cervantes
> Saavedra, *Don Quixote of la Mancha,* trans. Walter Starkie [New York:
> New American Library, 1957], 17.)

30. John T. Noonan, Jr., *The Lustre of Our Country: The American Experience
of Religious Freedom* (Berkeley: University of California Press, 1998), 265–284,
provides an excellent brief overview of the French Revolution and religion.

31. Modern discussion of the development of the First Amendment sometimes treats the subject as if the Framers approached the subject of religion as
did the French Revolutionaries, in an ideological manner, rather than applying
their principles and beliefs to contemporary problems and controversies, as if
"Somehow a set of definitive meanings was locked into the Constitution at the
moment of its adoption, presumably because the Framers (and Ratifiers) already possessed a sufficient body of materials and experiences on which to
form their final judgments." Jack N. Rakove, "Fidelity through History (or to
It)," *Fordham Law Review* 65 (1997): 1608.

32. See, for example, Mark S. Massa, *Catholics and American Culture* (New
York: Crossroad, 1999), 1–20; Joseph A. Varacalli, *Bright Promises, Failed Community: Catholics and the American Public Order* (Lanham, Mo.: Lexington Books,

2000). On American Catholicism, see John Tracy Ellis, *American Catholicism* (Chicago: University of Chicago Press, 1969); Jay P. Dolan, *The American Catholic Experience: A History from Colonial Times to the Present* (New York: Doubleday, 1985); James Hennesey, S.J., *American Catholics: A History of the Roman Catholic Community in the United States* (New York: Oxford University Press, 1981); Joseph F. Kelly, ed., *American Catholics* (Wilmington, Del.: Michael Glazier, 1989); Chester Gillis, *Roman Catholicism in America* (New York: Columbia University Press, 1999), 48–94.

33. Madison had initially opposed a Bill of Rights as "parchment" barriers against the will of a dominant majority. He thought the true guarantee of religious liberty lay in "the multiplicity of sects because there cannot be a majority of any one sect to oppress and persecute the rest." Jonathan Elliot, ed., *The Debates in the Several State Conventions on the Adoption of the Federal Constitution*, 5 vols. (Washington, D.C., 1936), 3:330.

34. Noonan, *Lustre of Our Country*, 6.

35. On neutrality, see Douglas Laycock, "Formal, Substantive, and Disaggregated Neutrality towards Religion," *DePaul Law Review* 39 (1990): 993–1018, and "The Remnants of Free Exercise," *Supreme Court Review* (1991): 16–17; Stephen V. Monsma, "Substantive Neutrality as a Basis for Free Exercise-No Establishment Common Ground," *Journal of Church and State* 42 (2000): 13–35. The present work holds that to allow the government to decide what encourages or discourages religious belief or practice is to endow government with power to determine and define religion.

36. *Everson v. Board of Education*, 330 U.S. 1, 31–32 (1947), and *School District of Abington Township v. Schempp*, 374 U.S. 203, 217 (1963). Carl H. Esbeck, "Table of United States Supreme Court Decisions Relating to Religious Liberty 1789–1994," *Journal of Law and Religion* 10 (1993–1994): 573–588, provides a summary of Church-State decisions, as does Witte, *Religion and the American Constitution*, 252–282. The *Religious Freedom Reporter*, published monthly, reviews a very wide range of cases and topics dealing with Church and State.

37. *Church of Lukumi v. Hialeah*, 508 U.S. 574 (1993). See Carl H. Esbeck, "Differentiating the Free Exercise and Establishment Clauses," *Journal of Church and State* 42 (2000): 323–324, for a different argument for why there is no conflict between the Free Exercise and No Establishment provisions.

38. Several authors, such as Leo Pfeffer, "The Unity of the First Amendment Religion Clauses," in *The First Freedoms: Religion and the Bill of Rights*, ed. James E. Wood, Jr. (Waco, Tex.: J. M. Dawson Institute of Church-State Studies at Baylor University, 1990), 133–166; Philip B. Kurland, *Religion and the Law: Of Church and State and the Supreme Court* (Chicago: Aldine, 1962); and John T. Noonan, Jr., "The End of Free Exercise?" *DePaul Law Review* 42 (1992): 567–582, have dealt with the First Amendment from a unitary standpoint. However, the focus of these works has been the effect of the amendment on religion, whereas the focus of the present book is on the effect of the

amendment on government. Smith, *Foreordained Failure,* 18, argues that the amendment was enacted for the single purpose of denying the federal government jurisdiction over religion so that the states could exercise such authority. He argues correctly that at the federal level it is pointless to try to determine "the meaning and scope of the principle of religious freedom" in the Constitution. The First Amendment keeps government out of religion so that people can define religious freedom for themselves. However, to assert that the amendment was enacted to guarantee the states' authority in religious matters is to argue that the states are capable of achieving in religion what the federal government is not. The thesis that the amendment was intended to confirm states' power over religion is incompatible with the historical development of religious liberty in America from the time of Roger Williams through William Penn and through the Evangelicals who emerged from the Great Awakening. They all believed that religious truth could only emerge if believers were free from government jurisdiction in religious matters. Too often, they had experienced governments' promotion of "dead" churches and "unconverted" ministers. The First Amendment arose out of a desire on the part of those who wanted a specific assurance that the federal government would not attempt to usurp the power over religion that they believed they had already denied to their own state governments.

2. The Formation of the First Amendment

1. John Witte, Jr., *Religion and the American Constitutional Experiment: Essential Rights and Liberties* (Boulder, Colo.: Westview Press, 2000), 7–20, provides a brief survey of Christendom.

2. On English Puritanism, see W. K. Jordan, *The Development of Religious Toleration in England,* 4 vols. (Cambridge: Harvard University Press, 1932–1940), and Carl Bridenbaugh, *Vexed and Troubled Englishmen, 1542–1642* (New York: Oxford University Press, 1968).

3. J. P. Kenyon, ed., *The Stuart Constitution 1603–1688: Documents and Commentary* (Cambridge: Cambridge University Press, 1966). For the Act of Toleration, see E. N. Williams, ed., *The Eighteenth-Century Constitution, 1688–1815: Documents and Commentary* (Cambridge: Cambridge University Press, 1962). The Act did not extend to Roman Catholics or non-Christians.

4. William Lee Miller, *The First Liberty: Religion and the American Republic* (New York: Alfred A. Knopf, 1986): 151–224; Timothy L. Hall, *Separating Church and State: Roger Williams and Religious Liberty* (Urbana: University of Illinois Press, 1998); Thomas J. Curry, *The First Freedoms: Church and State in America to the Passage of the First Amendment* (New York: Oxford University Press, 1986), 15–21, 91, 112.

5. Anson Phelps Stokes, *Church and State in the United States,* 3 vols. (New York: Harper & Brothers, 1950), 1:206–208; Curry, *First Freedoms,* 73–77; William Penn, *The Witness of William Penn,* Fredrick B. Tolles and E. Gordon

Alderfer eds. (New York: Macmillan, 1957); Hugh S. Barbour, ed. *William Penn on Religion and Ethnic: The Emergence of Liberal Quakerism,* 2 vols. (Lewiston: E. Mellon Press, 1991), 1: 393–490.

6. William G. McLoughlin, *New England Dissent 1630–1833: Baptists and the Separation of Church and State,* 2 vols. (Cambridge: Harvard University Press, 1971), 1: 329–491; Curry, *First Freedoms,* 94–104.

7. *Prince George County Petition,* November 28, 1785. Petitions can be found in *Religious Petitions Presented to the General Assembly of Virginia, 1774–1802* (Virginia State Library, microfilm, 3 vols.).

To the Honourable, the Speaker, and Gentlemen of the House of Delegates The petition of the Inhabitants of Prince George County Humbly Sheweth That whereas it hath Pleased your Honourable House to publish a Bill obligeing the Inhabitants of this Common Wealth to pay the Teachers of the christian Religion, and have requested their opinion concerning it; Your petitioners therefore do most earnestly declare against it: believing it to be Contrary to the Spirit of the Gospel, & the Bill [of] Rights. Certain it is, that The Blessed auther of our Religion supported & mantained his Gospel in the world for Several hundred years, not only without the aid of civil power, but against all the powers of the Earth. The Excellent purity of its' precepts, & the unblamable Behaviour of its Ministers (with the devine Blessing) made its Way thru all opposition: nor was it better for the church when Constantine first established Christianity by human Law, tho, there was Rest from persecution. But how soon Was the church overun with Error, Superstition and Immorality. How little were Ministers then like what they were before either in principle or purity? but it is said that Religion is taking it's flight, & that Deism, with it's bainfull Influence is spreading over the State; If so, it must be owing to other causes and Not for want of Religious Establishment. Let your laws punish the Vices and Immoralities of the times, and let there not be wanting such men placed in authority who by their pious Examples shall recommend Religion: & by their Faithfullness shall scurge the Growing Vices of the age: Let Ministers manifest to the World that they are Inwardly moved by the Holy Ghost to take upon them that office: that they seek the Good of Mankind, and not worldly Interest: let Their Doctrine be scriptural & their Lives upright; then shall Religion (if Departed) speedily return, and Deism be put to open shame & it's dreaded Consequencies speedily removed.

But what valuable purpose would such assessment answer? would it Introduce any More useful and faithful Men into the Ministry? Surely not, those whom devine Grace hath called to that work, will esteem it their highest Honour to do his pleasure: on the contrary, it Might call in many Hirelings whose cheif Motive would be temporal Interest.—that religious Establishment & Government are Linked together and that the latter cannot stand without the former is something new: Witness the State of pensylvania wherein no such Establishment hath ever taken place: Their Government stands firm, & which of the neighbouring States hath better Members, of brighter Morrals & more upright Characters.

That it is against our bill of Rights, which sayes all men by Nature are born equally free, so that no person in this Commonwealth shall enjoy exclusive privileges or Emoluments, except for services rendered to the state, shall not those then who are not professors of the christian Religion, who are in the state at the passing of this Bill, and others who have been Invited since by the benefit held out, when they shall be obliged to support the Christian Religion, think That such an obligation is a Departure from the Spirit and meaning of it.

Finaly, if such Tax is against the Spirit of the Gospel, if Christ for Several Hundred years, not only without the aid of civil power, but against all the powers of Earth and Hell supported it; if Establishment has never been a Means of prospering the Gospel: if no more faithful Men would be introduced into the Ministry by it: if it would not revive decay'd Religion and stop the Growth of Deism: or Serve the purpose of Government: and if against the bill of Rights: which your petitioners believe: they trust the wisdom and uprightness of your Honourable House will leave them Intirely free in Matters of Religion and the manner of supporting it's Ministers: and they shall ever pray . . .

This petition, submitted in varied forms, gained 4,899 signatures compared to 1,522 for Madison's *Memorial and Remonstrance.* William T. Hutchinson et al., eds., *Papers of James Madison,* 17 vols. (Chicago: University of Chicago Press, 1962–) 8:295–298, provides figures on signatures. See Jack N. Rakove, *Original Meanings: Politics and the Making of the Constitution* (New York: Alfred A. Knopf, 1996), 311. H. J. Eckenrode, *Separation of Church and State in Virginia* (1910; reprint, New York: Da Capo Press, 1971), 95–96, gives a variation on the above petition submitted by Rockingham County. See Thomas E. Buckley, S.J., *Church and State in Revolutionary Virginia, 1776–1787* (Charlottesville: University of Virginia Press, 1977).

8. McLoughlin, *New England Dissent,* 1:603.

9. Oscar and Mary Handlin, eds., *The Popular Sources of Political Authority: Documents on the Massachusetts Constitution of 1780* (Cambridge: Harvard University Press, 1966), collects the responses of the towns. This work has been used little in modern Church-State writings. See John Witte, Jr., " 'A Mild and Equitable Establishment of Religion': John Adams and the Massachusetts Experiment," *Journal of Church and State* 41 (1999): 213–252.

10. McLoughlin, *New England Dissent,* provides a superb review of Church and State in New England.

11. During the colonial period, the answer to whether Congregationalism was established in Massachusetts depended on circumstances. When taunted

by Anglicans that the law carried the Church of England establishment throughout the colonies, Congregationalists made plain that they were preeminent and preferred in Massachusetts. When accused by the English government of setting up a preference for themselves, they argued that they were merely supporting religion according to the choice of the individual towns. See Curry, *First Freedoms,* 107–113, 116–117, 127–133.

12. Curry, *First Freedoms,* 107–118, 125–128, 130–133, 175–177; Mc-Loughlin, *New England Dissent,* 2:1189–1262.

13. *Engel v. Vitale,* 370 U.S. 421, 425 (1962), and repeated in *School District of Abington Township v. Schempp,* 374 U.S. 203, 221 (1963).

14. On the preferentialist/nonpreferentialist controversy, see Robert L. Cord, *Separation of Church and State: Historical Fact and Current Fiction* (New York: Lambeth Press, 1982), and a critique of that work by Douglas Laycock, "'Nonpreferential' Aid to Religion: A False Claim about Original Intent," *William & Mary Law Review* 27 (1986): 875–923. Cord asserts correctly that Americans at the time of the enactment of the First Amendment defined an establishment of religion as a government preference for one religion, sect, or religious tradition. All the evidence points to the fact that they agreed universally with this definition. It represented their experience, and it conforms to the nature of religion and the observed behavior of humankind. However, Cord departs from history by drawing a logical inference that when Americans prohibited preferential government assistance to one religion, they approved nonpreferential government assistance to all. There is no historical evidence whatsoever to support that hypothesis.

The strength of Laycock's work is that he acknowledges and attempts to resolve historical difficulties. He recognizes that the supposedly nonpreferential religious systems of the time were in fact preferential and seen as tyrannical by minorities. But he draws the same logical inference as Cord—that the outlawing of preferential assistance implied the legality of nonpreferential aid. Thus, one author argues that the Framers understood and implied support for government aid. The other argues that they also understood the concept of nonpreferential government assistance but that they prohibited it. In reality, the historical evidence demonstrates that they defined establishment as a government preference and nothing more. They neither implied support for nor opposition to nonpreferential support because they did not make that distinction. Laycock acknowledges that positing a distinction between preferential and nonpreferential government assistance raises great difficulty with regard to James Madison, in that it would put him in the position of supporting the nonpreferential government assistance to religion Cord argues for. This position is clearly at odds with everything else we know about Madison. However, the problem lies in projecting back into the minds of the Framers a logical distinction that did not exist. Madison referred to Virginia as having no "exclusive establishment" of religion. He proposed prohibiting the establishment of a "national religion." Late in his life, in opposing the provision of congressional chaplains, he noted that the Constitution "forbids everything like an establishment of a national religion." Elizabeth Fleet, ed., "Madison's 'Detached Memoranda,' " *William & Mary Quarterly* 3 (1946): 558. Logical but unhistorical assumptions brought to the debate have controlled the historical discussion.

15. Every state constitution described establishment of religion in terms of a government preference, and states that set up a religious system, such as Massachusetts, and those that did not, such as Delaware or New Jersey, did not differ in how they described establishment. Requests for an amendment to the Constitution protecting religion all used the language of preference to describe establishment. All utterances at the time described establishment in terms of preference. No historical evidence exists to validate the hypothesis that when members of the First Congress wanted to substitute language prohibiting the establishment of "any particular denomination," they were arguing for nonpreferential government sponsorship of religion. See Curry, *First Freedoms,* 209–217; and Leonard W. Levy, *The Establishment Clause: Religion and the First Amendment* (New York, Macmillan, 1994), 111–114.

16. Francis Newton Thorpe, ed., *The Federal and State Constitutions, Colonial Charters, and other Organic Laws of the States, Territories, and Colonies now or heretofore forming the United States of America,* 7 vols. (Washington, D.C.: Government Printing Office, 1909), 5:3100. See Chester James Antieau, Arthur T. Downey, and Edward C. Roberts, *Freedom from Federal Establishment: Formation and Early History of the First Amendment Religion Clauses* (Milwaukee: Bruce Publishing Co., 1964), 132–134, for references to establishment in state constitutions. Isaac Backus mistakenly thought that the First Amendment actually read that "Congress shall make no law, establishing articles of faith, or a mode of worship, or prohibiting the free exercise of religion," and he happily accepted such wording. McLoughlin, *New England Dissent,* 2:783–784. Backus believed that both Massachusetts and Connecticut acted contrary to it. In 1794, John Leland, a Baptist minister and one of the leaders of the Virginia movement for a federal Bill of Rights, proposed an amendment to the Massachusetts Constitution demanding that religion be supported on a voluntary basis. Yet he ended his proposal with the statement that the legislature should never "establish any religion by law, give any one sect a preference over another." L. F. Greene, ed., *The Writings of John Leland* (1854; reprint, New York: Arno Press, 1969), 229. According to the preferentialist/nonpreferentialist interpretation, these statements would put both in the nonpreferential camp as supporters of the Massachusetts Church-State system. However, both spent their lives fighting that system. The failure of modern scholarship to account for the thought and actions of such men as Madison, Backus, and Leland, who were the most involved in and informed about Church and State, constitutes undeniable proof that the present paradigm of Church-State discussion is in deep crisis. See Thomas S. Kuhn, *The Structure of Scientific Revolutions* (Chicago: University of Chicago Press, 1970), 66–91. The present historical method of

examining the history of the First Amendment can only survive by ignoring or discounting the relevant historical evidence.

17. Charles Francis Adams, ed., *The Works of John Adams,* 10 vols. (Boston: Little, Brown & Co., 1850–1856), 10:188. Curry, *First Freedoms,* 126–129.

18. Thorpe, *Federal and State Constitutions,* 3: 1274. See Stokes, *Church and State in the United States,* 1:444–445 for Jefferson as the author of this declaration.

19. McLoughlin, *New England Dissent,* 1:510–511.

20. These Bills are found in Buckley, *Church and State in Revolutionary Virginia,* 188–190.

21. See Eckenrode, *Separation of Church and State in Virginia.* Because the General Assessment controversy is discussed almost exclusively in terms of Madison's *Memorial and Remonstrance* and Jefferson's *Bill for Religious Liberty,* modern commentators miss both the overall context and atmosphere in which the controversy occurred and the evangelical fervor of the majority of its opponents.

22. *Cumberland County Petition,* November 6, 1778.

23. As part of a petition against General Assessment, the ministers of the Presbyterian Church wrote in 1785:

When the late happy Revolution secured to us exemption from British control, we hoped that the gloom of injustice and Usurpation would have been forever dispelled. . . . But our hopes have since been overcast with apprehensions when we found how slowly and unwillingly ancient distinctions among the citizens, on account of religions opinions, were removed by the Legislature. For although the glaring impartiality of obliging all denominations to support the one which had been the favorite of government was pretty early withdrawn, yet an evident predilection in favor of that church still subsisted in the acts of the Assembly. Peculiar distinctions and the honor of an important name was still continued; and these are considered as equally partial and injurious with the ancient emoluments. Our apprehension on account of the continuance of these, which could have no further effect than to produce jealous animosities and unnecessary contentions among different parties, were increased when we found that they were tenaciously adhered to by government, notwithstanding the remonstrances of several Christian societies. To increase the evil, a manifested disposition has been shown by the State to consider itself as possessed of supremacy in *spirituals* as well as *temporal;* and our fears have been realized in certain proceedings of the General Assembly at their last sessions. The ingrossed bill for establishing a provision for the teachers of the Christian religion, and the act for incorporating the Protestant Episcopal church, so far as it secures to that church the churches, glebes, etc., procured at the expense of the whole community, are not only evidences of this, but of an impolitic partiality which we are sorry to have observed so long. (Miscellaneous [Presbyter-ian] Petition (November 2, 1785), in *Documentary History of the Struggle for Religious Liberty in Virginia,* ed. Charles F. James [Lynchburg: J. P. Bell, 1900], 236.)

Maryland, too, debated and rejected a general state tax to aid religion, and present-day commentators have seen this as another example of a state choos-ing to see nondiscriminatory government aid to religion as a nonpreferential kind of establishment. However, even more than Virginians, the people of Maryland saw the plan as an attempt to restore a preference for the previously established Anglican Church, and they drew no distinction in their minds be-tween preferential and nonpreferential establishments or aid to religion. Curry, *First Freedoms,* 154–157.

24. See, for example, Steven D. Smith, *Foreordained Failure: The Quest for a Constitutional Principle of Religious Freedom* (New York: Oxford University Press, 1995), 18; Akil Reed Amar, "The Bill of Rights as a Constitution," *Yale Law Journal* 100 (1991): 1131, and *The Bill of Rights: Creation and Reconstruction* (New Haven: Yale University Press, 1998), 20–45; "Rethinking the Incorporation of the Establishment Clause; A Federalist View," *Harvard Law Review* 105 (1992): 1703, provides a bibliography of works espousing this viewpoint.

25. Jed Rubenfeld, "Antidisestablishmentarianism: Why RFRA Really Was Unconstitutional," *Michigan Law Review* 95 (1997): 2351, provides a listing of various modern counts of establishments of religion in America at the time of the enactment of the First Amendment. Justice John Paul Stevens, for ex-ample, in *County of Allegheny v. ACLU, Greater Pittsburgh Chapter,* 492 U.S. 573, 646 (1989), counted six state establishments. Amar, *Bill of Rights,* 32–33, men-tions six states as having a congregational or a "more general" establishment. However, South Carolina abandoned the last state establishment in 1790. Those who supported state religious systems did not define them as establish-ments. Massachusetts required that "no subordination of any one denomina-tion to another shall ever be established by law." Opponents of this system agreed with this definition of establishment. However, they opposed the sys-tem of state support because in their experience it was indeed preferential, co-ercive, and oppressive. It represented for them the establishment of one reli-gious group. At the time the First Amendment was enacted, those who supported the system and argued for government support for religion did not approve of establishment. Modern scholars have assigned nonhistorical con-cepts and terms such as "multiple" or "nonpreferential" establishment to the American past. They arrange the historical data according to this modern analysis and definition and then proceed to use that arrangement as "historical evidence" for the "original" understanding of "establishment of religion" and of the First Amendment. Massachusetts, for example, did not officially create an establishment in 1780, nor did it officially disestablish religion in 1833. However, most modern discussion of the matter assumes the state did both.

See Smith, *Foreordained Failure*, 48, for a statement noting that scholars some-times define the "original meaning" they supposedly are seeking.

26. See Curry, *First Freedoms*, 134–192.

27. "Traditionalists could support the amendment precisely because it pro-hibited the national government from interfering with states like Massachu-setts and Connecticut that adhered to the traditional position favoring estab-lished religion." Smith, *Foreordained Failure*, 21. Of the states that implemented or permitted a state religious system—Massachusetts, Connecticut, New Hampshire, and Georgia—only New Hampshire ratified the First Amend-ment at the time. Neither Massachusetts nor Connecticut proposed an amend-ment regarding religion. No state—apart from South Carolina until 1790—proclaimed an establishment of religion, and all would have denied vigorously that they did, particularly within the meaning of the First Amendment. Just prior to the Revolution, Americans had fiercely opposed a proposal to intro-duce Anglican bishops to America, because they saw this move as setting up an establishment of religion. Charles Chauncy, a spokesman for Congregational-ist New England, vigorously denounced a "STATE ESTABLISHMENT." Curry, *First Freedoms*, 172, 211. The argument in Amar, *Bill of Rights*, 41, that "the amendment was indeed agnostic on the issue of establishment" is fanciful in that no one in America at the time defended an establishment of religion and all wanted to disassociate themselves from that concept. Supporters of the General Assessment in Virginia were careful to distance themselves from ad-vocating an establishment. They argued that the assessment was fair, equitable, and preferred none, that is, that it was not an establishment. Similarly, propo-nents of the religious systems in Massachusetts and Connecticut argued that these systems did not fall within the agreed upon definition of establishment. Opponents argued that they certainly did. See Leonard W. Levy, "The Bill of Rights," *The American Founding: Essays on the Formation of the Constitution*, ed. J. Jackson Barlow, Leonard, W. Levy, and Ken Masugi (New York: Greenwood Press, 1988), 31, for a discussion on the Massachusetts response to the First Amendment.

28. According to the "federalism" argument, the First Amendment pre-vented the federal government from coercion in religion but preserved the ability of the states to maintain establishments. However, since proponents of the New England Church-State systems did not agree that they were estab-lishments, this provision would have been of little use to them. No group in America at the time would have defended an establishment of religion. The "federalism" argument belongs entirely to the world of logical distinctions and has no connection with the world of history.

29. *Annals of Congress*, 1:757–759.

30. See Curry, *First Freedoms*, 194–198. Modern discussion of the origins of the First Amendment has largely failed to appreciate its evangelical roots. This is a result, in part, of concentrating on Madison's *Memorial and Remon-strance* at the expense of the other petitions. It has also resulted in a failure to

understand how much Pennsylvania provided a role model for religious liberty. See Merrill Jensen et al., eds., *The Documentary History of the Ratification of the Constitution,* 18 vols. (Madison: State Historical Society of Wisconsin, 1976-), 2:288, 386, 392, 399–400, 459, 467, 514, 597, 623. Comments from Pennsylvania regarding a Bill of Rights focused on the need to protect liberty of conscience.

31. The incorporation of the First Amendment by way of the Fourteenth Amendment is entirely in accord with the development and emergence of religious liberty in America. States increasingly took away power to make decisions in religious matters from their governments. In dismantling of establishments of religion where they existed, and in demanding that religion be a voluntary exercise, most states made enormous strides in this effort. In the decades following the ratification of the Constitution, the New England states belatedly joined this movement. In denying the federal government authority in religion, the states were only doing what they themselves had done. It is entirely consistent with history that the liberty guaranteed by the Fourteenth Amendment should include freedom from any government exercise of power in religion.

32. See Jon Butler, *Awash in a Sea of Faith* (Cambridge: Harvard University Press, 1990), 258–259; John T. Noonan, Jr., *The Believer and the Powers That Are* (New York: Macmillan, 1987), 127. "Even in the arguably 'no establishment' states, church and state were hardly separate." Amar, *Bill of Rights,* 33.

33. McLoughlin, *New England Dissent,* 1:606–607; Curry, *First Freedoms,* 221–222.

3. The Continuing Emergence of Religious Liberty

1. John T. Noonan, Jr. *The Lustre of Our Country: The American Experience of Religious Freedom* (Berkeley: University of California Press, 1998), 265–284.

2. *Everson v. Board of Education,* 330 U.S. 1, 15 (1947). This metaphor had been cited by the Court in *Reynolds v. United States,* 98 U.S. 145, 164 (1878).

3. "Believing with you that religion is a matter which lies solely between man and his God; that he owes account to none other for his faith or his worship; that the legislative powers of the Government reach actions only, and not opinions, I contemplate with sovereign reverence that act of the whole American people which declared that their Legislature should 'make no law respecting an establishment of religion or prohibiting the free exercise thereof,' thus building a wall of separation between Church and State." In Anson Phelps Stokes, *Church and State in the United States,* 3 vols. (New York: Harper & Brothers, 1950), 1:335.

4. *Pierce v. Society of Sisters,* 268 U.S. 510 (1925), upheld the right to operate parochial schools.

5. Letter to Reverend Samuel Miller, in Stokes, *Church and State,* 1:490.

6. *McDaniel v. Paty,* 435 U.S. 618 (1978).

7. Stokes, *Church and State,* 1:483–517; Chester James Antieau, Arthur T. Downey, and Edward C. Roberts, *Freedom from Federal Establishment: Formation and Early History of the First Amendment Religion Clauses* (Milwaukee: Bruce Publishing. 1964), 159–200.

8. *Federalist Papers,* 2.

9. Martin Marty, "Living with Establishment and Disestablishment in Nineteenth-Century Anglo-America," *Journal of Church and State* 18 (1976): 73. See also Martin Marty, *Protestantism in the United States: Righteous Empire* (New York: Scribner's, 1986); Robert T. Handy, *A Christian America: Protestant Hopes and Historical Realities* (New York: Oxford University Press, 1984), and other works by the same author; Morton Border, *Jews, Turks, and Infidels* (Chapel Hill: University of North Carolina Press, 1984); and Joyce Appleby, *Inheriting the Revolution: The First Generation of Americans* (Cambridge: Harvard University Press, 2000), 194–266.

10. *Annals of Congress,* 1:914–915; L. F. Greene, ed., *Writings of John Leland* (1854; reprint, New York: Arno Press, 1969), 107.

11. *Annals of Congress,* 1:758.

12. See Andrew M. Greeley, *The Catholic Imagination* (Berkeley: University of California Press, 2000), and many other writings on Catholicism by the same author. R. Lawrence Moore, *Religious Outsiders and the Making of Americans* (New York: Oxford University Press, 1986), 48–71, discusses Catholicism in nineteenth-century America.

13. Patrick J. Dignan, *A History of Legal Incorporation of the Catholic Church in the United States (1784–1932)* (New York: J. P. Kenedy & Sons, 1935).

14. Patrick W. Carey, *People, Priests, and Prelates: Ecclesiastical Democracy and the Tensions of Trusteeism* (Notre Dame, Ind.: University of Notre Dame Press, 1987); "Republicanism within American Catholicism, 1785–1860," *Journal of the Early Republic* 3 (1983): 413–437; and "The Laity's Understanding of the Trustee System, 1785–1855," *Catholic Historical Review* 64 (1978): 357–376.

15. The Boston case can be found in Mark De Wolfe Howe, ed., *Cases on Church and State in the United States* (Cambridge: Harvard University Press, 1952).

16. Timothy L. Smith, "Protestant Schooling and Nationality," *Journal of American History* 53 (1966–1967): 679–695; "Immigrant Social Aspirations and American Education, 1880–1930," *American Quarterly* 21 (1969): 523–543; *Revivalism and Social Reform in Mid-Nineteenth Century America* (New York: Harper & Row, 1957); James C. Carper, "A Common Faith for the Common School? Religion and Education in Kansas, 1861–1900," *Mid-America* 60 (1978):147–161; Robert S. Michaelsen, *Piety in the Public School: Trends and Issues in the Relationship between Religion and the Public School in the United States* (New York: Macmillan, 1970).

17. Philip Schaff, *Church and State in the United States* (1888; reprint, New York: Arno Press, 1972), 72.

18. Ray Allen Billington, *The Protestant Crusade, 1800–1860: A Study of the Origins of American Nativism* (New York: Macmillan, 1938). John Higham, *Strangers in the Land: Patterns of American Nativism, 1860–1925* (New York: Atheneum, 1969).

19. Justice Rehnquist's dissent is found in *Wallace v. Jaffree,* 472 U.S. 38, 91–114 (1985).

20. By using this wording, supporters of the General Assessment were arguing that they were preserving the free exercise of religion without creating an establishment of religion, that is, they were not creating a "pre-eminence" for any one group. All at the time opposed an establishment of religion.

21. *Federalist Papers* 51.

22. *Wallace v. Jaffree,* 472 U.S. 38, 113 (1985).

23. Richard John Neuhaus, *The Naked Public Square* (Grand Rapids: Wm. B. Eerdmans, 1984). See also *First Things: A Journal of Religion and Public Life,* edited by Neuhaus. *The Naked Public Square* cloaks Church-State discussion in metaphorical, indefinable language that obscures an essential distinction. The First Amendment protects the practice and expression of religion in public places, parks, streets, and buildings controlled by government. The same amendment forbids government to sponsor religious devotion or practice, to compose or decide on religious exercises to erect religious symbols, or to legislate religious actions.

24. See Noonan, *Lustre of our Country,* 331–352, for developments in Catholic Church-State thought. For the text of the *Declaration,* see Austin Flattery, O.P., ed., *Vatican Council II: The Conciliar Documents and Post Conciliar Documents* (Collegeville, Minn.: Liturgical Press, 1975), 799–812. The *Declaration* is also available online at many sites and can be found under its Latin title, *Dignitatis Humanae.*

25. Flannery, *Vatican Council II,* 802.

26. This viewpoint, that the First Amendment prohibits only religious discrimination, is often expressed in Amicus Curiae briefs submitted to the Supreme Court by the United States Catholic Conference. See, for example, the brief in *Guy Mitchell, et al., v. Mary L. Helms, et al.,* (August 19, 1999).

27. Schaff, *Church and State in the United States,* 73.

28. See Charles R. Morris, *American Catholic: The Saints and Sinners Who Built America's Most Powerful Church* (New York: Random House, 1997), for an excellent overview of Catholicism in America. The author masters and reflects the current body of American Catholic scholarship but stays within the assimilationist tradition.

29. John T. Ellis, "American Catholics and the Intellectual Life," *Thought* 30 (1955): 351–388.

30. In Catholic teaching before the Second Vatican Council, abstract reasoning and logic tended to predominate over history and experience. Ironically, this logical approach continues to exercise great influence in Catholic thinking on Church and State. For example, Chester James Antieau, Arthur T.

Downey, and Edward C. Roberts, *Freedom from Federal Establishment: Formation and Early History of the First Amendment Religion Clauses* (Milwaukee: Bruce Publishing Co., 1964), sets out to dispose of the Supreme Court's interpretation of the First Amendment by proving that government could sponsor religion on a nonpreferential basis. The work provides much useful historical data, but it is arranged logically, rather than historically or chronologically, in order to support a series of logical propositions.

31. *Federalist Papers* 51, 75.

4. The End of Christendom and the Role of the Courts

1. This work argues throughout for the recovery of the religious and evangelical roots of the First Amendment. This is not to deny the influence of the Enlightenment in the formation of the amendment. Many of the enduring statements about religious liberty were written by those who were indeed influenced greatly by Enlightenment thinking. However, it was the American religious and evangelical background of religious liberty that made the American experience of it unique. For an examination of how Enlightenment thinking developed with regard to religious liberty, one needs to look to France rather than to America.

2. *Watson v. Jones* 80 U.S. 679, 728–729 (1871).

3. See *Jones v. Wolf*, 443 U.S. 579, 612 (1979), for a list of cases involving disputes over church property. See also Kent Greenwalt, "Hands Off! Civil Court Involvement in Conflicts over Religious Property," *Columbia Law Review* 98 (1998): 1843–1907.

4. See *Presbyterian Church in the United States v. Mary Elizabeth Blue Hull Memorial Presbyterian Church*, 393 U.S. 440 (1969) in which the Supreme Court forbade a state to look into the issue of implied trust.

5. *Jones v. Wolf*, 443 U.S. 595, 596, 602–606 (1979).

6. See Carl H. Esbeck, "Table of United States Supreme Court Decisions Relating to Religious Liberty 1789–1994," *Journal of Law and Religion* 10 (1993–1994): 573–588; and John Witte, Jr., *Religion and the American Constitutional Experiment: Essential Rights and Liberties* (Boulder, Colo.: Westview Press, 2000), 251–282, for a summary of cases.

7. *Cox v. New Hampshire*, 312 U.S. 569 (1941).

8. *Poulos v. New Hampshire* 345 U.S. 395 (1953) deals with the Portsmouth ordinance.

9. *Joseph Burstyn, Inc. v. Wilson* 343 U.S. 306 (1952); *Torcaso v. Watkins* 367 U.S. 488 (1961).

10. *McCollum v. Board of Education*, 333 U.S. 203 (1948); *Engel v. Vitale*, 370 U.S. 421 (1962); *School District of Abington Township v. Schempp*, 374 U.S. 203 (1963); *Edwards v. Aguillard* 482 U.S. 578 (1987); *Stone v. Graham*, 449 U.S. 39 (1980); *Wallace v. Jaffree*, 472 U.S. 38 (1985); *Lee v. Weisman*, 505 U.S. 577 (1992); *Santa Fe Independent School District v. Jane Doe* [June 19, 2000].

11. See Luke 6:20–31; John 13:34.

12. See "School District Is Sued after Poster Is Censored," *New York Times*, November 3, 1999.

13. See *County of Allegheny v. ACLU, Greater Pittsburgh Chapter*, 492 U.S. 573, 657 (1989).

14. *Zorach v. Clauson*, 343 U.S. 306, 312 (1952).

15. The three-part test is found in *Lemon v. Kurtzman*, 403 U.S. 602, 612–613 (1971). Chief Justice Rehnquist's dissenting opinion in *Santa Fe Independent School District v. Jane Doe* [June 19, 2000] criticizes this test and provides a guide to other judicial critiques of it.

16. The announcement of the decision in *County of Allegheny v. ACLU, Greater Pittsburgh Chapter*, 492 U.S. 573 (1989) is illustrative of the inability of the Court to find a common approach:

> BLACKMUN, J., announced the judgment of the Court and delivered the opinion of the Court with respect to Parts III-A, IV, and V, in which BRENNAN, MARSHALL, STEVENS, and O'CONNOR, JJ., joined; an opinion with respect to Parts I and II, in which STEVENS, O'CONNOR, JJ., joined; an opinion with respect to Part III-B, in which STEVENS, J., joined; an opinion with respect to Part VII, in which O'CONNOR, J., joined; and an opinion with respect to Part VI. O'CONNOR, J., filed an opinion concurring in part, and concurring in the judgment, in Part II of which BRENNAN and STEVENS, JJ., joined, post, p. 623. BRENNAN, J., filed an opinion concurring in part and dissenting in part, in which MARSHALL and STEVENS, JJ., joined, post, p. 637. STEVENS, J., filed an opinion concurring in part and dissenting in part, in which BRENNAN, and MARSHALL, JJ., joined, post, p. 646. KENNEDY, J., filed an opinion concurring in the judgment in part and dissenting in part, in which REHNQUIST, C. J., and WHITE, and SCALIA, JJ., joined. . . .

17. *Widmar v. Vincent*, 454 U.S. 263 (1981).

18. *Bd. of Educ. of Westside Community Schools v. Mergens*, 496 U.S. 226 (1990).

19. *Lamb's Chapel v. Center Moriches Union Free School District*, 508 U.S. 384 (1993).

20. *Church of the Lukumi Babalu Aye, Inc. v. City of Hialeah*, 508 U.S. 520 (1993).

21. *Texas Monthly, Inc. v. Bullock*, 489 U.S. 1 (1989).

22. *Larkin v. Grendel's Den*, 459 U.S. 116 (1982).

23. *Kiryas Joel Village School District v. Grumet*, 512 U.S. 687 (1994).

24. *Marsh v. Chambers*, 463 U.S. 783, 792 (1983).

25. *Lynch v. Donnelly*, 465 U.S. 668, 683 (1984), and *County of Allegheny v. ACLU, Greater Pittsburgh Chapter*, 492 U.S. 573 (1989).

26. *Lyng v. Northwest Indian Cemetery Protective Ass'n*, 485 U.S. 439, 457–458 (1988).

27. *Capital Square Review and Advisory Board v. Pinette* 515 U.S. 753 (1995).

28. See Esbeck, "Table of United States Supreme Court Decisions," and Witte, *Religion and the American Constitutional Experiment,* for a summary of these cases. In June 2000, the Court decided *Mitchell et al. v. Helms,* which dealt with the provision of educational materials and equipment, including computer equipment, to parochial schools. This decision modified some of the Court's previous rulings. It can serve well as an example of the impenetrable nature of modern Court opinions that results from the inability of the justices to agree on a rationale that connects with the history and purpose of the First Amendment. In his dissent, Justice David Souter continued to exemplify the fundamental error of mistaking Virginia's historic refusal to give its government power to enact religious legislation (paying ministers at public expense to preach) as authorizing modern judges to evaluate the possible religious consequences of secular legislation. The function of courts is to assess whether government is exceeding its delegated powers by making decisions in religious matters, wherein it is powerless. Judges have neither authority nor competence to assess the possible religious consequences of secular laws. Failure to make this distinction perpetuates the confusion about the meaning of the First Amendment that has engulfed the Court's Church-State decisions. The impact of secular legislation on churches is for their members to decide. The same confusion underlies Justice Souter's statement that "government aid corrupts religion." Those who contributed to the development of the free exercise of religion argued that government legislation in religious issues—what Roger Williams called the First Table—would indeed corrupt religion. Paying ministers to preach is an example of such legislation. Whether participating in a secular government program will corrupt religion is again for believers to decide. Judges are not the guardians of religious purity. To put them in the position of evaluating all laws using a religious standard would be to endow them with enormous and unlimited authority and to attempt to make secular judges and legislators experts in religious matters.

29. *Lemon v. Kurtzman,* 403 U.S. 602, 610 (1971). See *To Teach as Jesus Did: A Pastoral Message on Catholic Education* (Washington, D.C.: National Conference of Catholic Bishops, 1972).

30. *National Labor Relations Board v. The Catholic Bishop of Chicago,* 440 U.S. 490 (1979).

31. *Bd. of Educ. v. Allen,* 392 U.S. 236, 238–249 (1968).

32. *Lemon v. Kurtzman,* 403 U.S. 602, 635–636 (1971).

33. Justice Douglas referred to the supporters of parochial schools as "dissenters." Ibid., 629.

34. "It is hardly a lack of due process for Government to regulate that which it subsidizes." *Wickard v. Filburn,* 317 U.S. 111, 131 (1942); *Bob Jones University v. United States,* 461 U.S. 574 (1983).

35. *Agostini v. Felon,* 521 U.S. 230 (1997).

36. *Jackson v. Benson,* 578 N.W. 2d 602 (1998).

37. See David R. Manwaring, *Render unto Caesar: The Flag-salute Controversy* (Chicago: University of Chicago Press, 1962).

38. *Minersville School District v. Gobitis,* 310 U.S. 586, 591 (1940).

39. *West Virginia State Board of Education v. Barnette,* 319 U.S. 624, 642 (1943).

40. Ibid., 646.

41. *Sherbert v. Verner,* 374 U.S. 398, 403 (1963).

42. *Employment Division v. Smith,* 494 U.S. 872 (1990).

43. For historical exceptions to swearing oaths, see Thomas J. Curry, *The First Freedoms: Church and State in America to the Passage of the First Amendment* (New York: Oxford University Press, 1986), 81. See Michael McConnell, "The Origins and Historical Understanding of Free Exercise of Religion," *Harvard Law Review* 103 (1990): 1410, for a comprehensive examination of this issue. However, see also Philip A. Hamburger, "A Constitutional Right to Religious Exemption: An Historical Perspective," *George Washington Law Review* 60 (1992): 915.

44. *Gonzalez v. Archbishop,* 280 U.S. 1, 16–17 (1929).

45. Esbeck, "Table of United States Supreme Court Decisions," and Witte, *Religion and the American Constitutional Experiment,* 252–282, provide a summary of the cases following.

46. *Capitol Square Review and Advisory Board v. Pinette* 515 U.S. 753 (1995).

47. *Lee v. Weisman,* 505 U.S. 507, 646 (1992).

48. *Marsh v. Chambers,* 463 U.S. 783 (1983).

49. *Lynch v. Donnelly,* 464 U.S. 668, 687 (1984).

50. *Bradfield v. Roberts,* 175 U.S. 291 (1899).

Conclusion

1. *Everson v. Board of Education,* 330 U.S. 1, 34 (1947).

2. *Annals of Congress,* 1:758.

3. *School District of Abington Township v. Schempp,* 374 U.S. 203, 233 (1963). An overemphasis on persecution leads to the view of the First Amendment as an exercise in pragmatism as "articles of peace in a pluralist society." John Courtney Murray, S.J., *We Hold These Truths* (Kansas City, Mo.: Sheed & Ward, 1960), 78. See Akhil Reed Amar, *The Bill of Rights: Creation and Reconstruction* (New Haven: Yale University Press, 1998), 34, comparing the First Amendment to the Peace of Augsburg in 1555 and the Treaty of Westphalia of 1648. For America, the Act of Toleration had brought religious peace a century before the Bill of Rights.

4. *City of Bourne v. Flores,* 521 U.S. 507, 541–542 (1997). The *Memorial and Remonstrance* stated:

Because finally, "the equal right of every citizen to the free exercise of his Religion according to the dictates of conscience" is held by the same tenure with all our other rights. If we recur to its origin, it is equally the gift of nature; if we weigh its importance, it cannot be less dear to us; if we consult the "Declaration of those rights which pertain to the good people of Virginia, as the basis and foundation of Government," it is enumerated with equal solemnity, or rather studied emphasis.

5. See J. R. Bartlett, ed., *Records of the Colony of Rhode Island and Providence Plantations in New England 1632–1792,* 10 vols. (Providence: A. C. Greene, 1856–65), 1:287, for comment about tithes. See Leonard W. Levy, "No Establishment of Religion: The Original Understanding," in Leonard W. Levy, *Judgments: Essays on American Constitutional History* (Chicago: Quadrangle Books, 1972), 177, for Rhode Island's proposed amendment.

6. *County of Allegheny v. ACLU, Greater Pittsburgh Chapter,* 492 U.S. 573, 664 (1989).

INDEX

Unitarians, 32

Virginia, 14
  Bill of Rights, 29, 40
  and Christendom, 29, 30
  and General Assessment, 29–30,
    39–41, 123 n. 7, 127 n. 23,
    135 n. 28
  religious liberty in, 28–30
Vouchers, 91–92

Wall of separation
  as conferring power on
    government, 19, 21, 79–80,
    82–82, 90, 104, 113–114
  critics of Court and, 52, 59

and French Revolution, 47, 50
and ideology, 4, 88
inadequacy of, 84, 87, 108
incompatible with Court
  decisions, 75
and Thomas Jefferson, 48,
  130 n. 3
unhistorical, 49
Wall, Thomas, 56, 59
Wars of Religion, 16, 24, 80
Washington, George, 40
White, Justice Byron, 87
Williams, Roger, on religious liberty,
  25–26, 34, 43, 107, 112, 135
  n. 28
Wisconsin voucher program, 91